MYSTERY MUSES

100 Classics That Inspire Today's Mystery Writers

edited by
Jim Huang & Austin Lugar

THE CRUM CREEK PRESS
Carmel, Indiana

Acknowledgments

The editors would like to acknowledge the invaluable assistance of Dotty Bonadies, Sherry Crane, Moni Draper, Phil Dunlap, Jennie Jacobson, Jeanne Jacobson, Jaci Muzamel, Jen Roth, Carla Schaaf and Larry Sweazy in the preparation of this book.

MYSTERY MUSES

ISBN: 0-9625804-9-X

First edition: November 2006

Cover art by Robin Agnew (Aunt Agatha's, Ann Arbor, MI)
Cover design by Patricia Prather

Index by Larry Sweazy

"The Edgar" and "The Edgar Allan Poe Award" are service marks of The Mystery Writers of America.

The Crum Creek Press
484 East Carmel Drive #378
Carmel, IN 46032

www.crumcreekpress.com

Contents

Introduction

What inspires a mystery writer?

We asked 100 published writers: "Did a mystery set you on your path to being a writer? Is there a classic mystery that remains important to you today?" This book is the result.

The writers we contacted represent the entire spectrum of the mystery genre, from cozy to hardboiled, from acclaimed veterans to some of the field's most intriguing newcomers. Young or old, each of these writers reminds us of a basic truism: great writers are great readers first. Their essays reveal the extent to which the discovery of these seminal texts was not just literary inspiration but a life-altering event.

We found it especially endearing to see how often contributors referred not just to a book's text but to its literal form as well: a particular copy of a particular edition. We are reminded that the power of the printed word derives in part from the fact that it is printed and bound, fixed in both time and place.

In these essays, we're also reminded of the power of the genre itself. For many writers, their classics represent more than just a bar against which to measure their own work. These classics inspired a new way to look at the landscape of literature.

These writers represent several generations of mystery lovers, and the classics they cite represent every era of the mystery story, from the 1840s to the 1990s. We've arranged these essays in the order of the publication of the classics they cover, from Edgar Allan Poe's "The Cask of the Amontillado" to Dennis Lehane's *Gone, Baby, Gone*. This chronological arrangement offers something of a history of the genre, and reveals that the virtues of early crime stories are not necessarily the same as what we admire in more recent work.

It's striking how many of the classics covered are newer. Fifty essays cover books published in 1952 and earlier. Fifty essays cover books published since 1954. Can a book that's just 25 years old be considered a classic? Just 10 years old? Our position is simple: just because a book was published recently doesn't mean it didn't influence someone. The power of a story doesn't derive from its age; it's in the story itself, and its reader.

If genre truly is "a conversation among texts," as science fiction editor David Hartwell has written, we hope that *Mystery Muses* will become part of the conversation. These essays are not just about 100 beloved books. They are just as much about 100 of the genre's finest current practitioners, writers who respect the past and who continue to be inspired by classics as they define the future of the mystery story.

— *Jim Huang & Austin Lugar*

Mystery Muses

Rob Kantner on
The Cask of Amontillado by Edgar Allan Poe (1843)

When I was just eight, my grandfather lent me a collection of Poe stories. He cautioned me that the tales — especially "The Tell-Tale Heart" — were creepy and scary. No doubt he was concerned about the impact of such dark, dreamy, almost delirious fiction on a young innocent mind. It had an effect, all right. But not the one my grandfather feared. And "Heart" was not the tale that clung. It's "The Cask of Amontillado" that's stuck with me these 40 plus years. Not just for its psychological impact, but as an exemplar of technique. It's spare (barely 2300 words), unsparing, hardboiled, ingenious. It carves out its own space and fills that space brilliantly. Through it Poe continues to teach lessons in craftsmanship that have, I now find, influenced my work more than once.

Take the exposition, such as it is. In just 100-plus words, Poe gets the job done. Montresor, the protagonist, vows revenge on one Fortunato. Not, he claims, because of "the thousand injuries" Fortunato inflicted, but because the man "ventured on insult." This opening generates immediate suspense because it raises many more questions than it answers. What form will the revenge take? And what was the insult? Is it possible there wasn't one? That Montresor is, perhaps, unreliable?

Because we want answers, we continue to read. Poe has met the first narrative test: to drag the reader past the beginning.

Swiftly he brings Montresor to life, as he leads the unfortunate Fortunato to his death. Though the exposition frames the tale as a confessional, we get to know Montresor not so much by what he says, but by witnessing what he does, how he does it, and how he feels about it. How he feels is — save an odd instant at the end — triumphant. He struts and brags and crows in the best of what has become the hardboiled tradition.

For all of that, Poe veils the outcome. Until we get to the end, we don't see it coming. To create and sustain suspense without telegraphing the outcome is so tough to do. As familiar as this tale is by now, it's easy to take for granted the intricacy of the building blocks by which Poe builds suspense, sustains it and then socks the reader at the end.

I doubt that any other piece of fiction has influenced my own work — at best pale and imitative — quite so much.

"Fly Away Home" — which won the Shamus — is also a hardboiled confessional. It also almost completely lacks exposition. Like Montresor, the narrator is a murderer, the victim of insult, unreliable. He too is clever, though not as clever as Montresor: in the end my guy gets his.

"Crooked Lake" (Alfred Hitchcock's Mystery Magazine, 2005) is another first-person, by another unnamed narrator. Like Montresor, he takes revenge. But his cause is less ignoble: his target killed the love of his life. Like Montresor, the narrator's plan exploits his target's weakness (in his case, a terminal need to feel accepted). Like Montresor, he gets away with it.

And my protagonist, like Montresor, has obviously monitored for decades the place where rest his victim's bones. I remember that as I wrote the final sentences in which this becomes plain, the words from Poe's pen echoed in my head: "for the half of a century no mortal has disturbed them."

Clearly, as I wrote my concluding words, I was in large part sending them out to wherever the soul of that tortured genius resides. It was a tip of my hat to the old master. May he rest in peace!

Besides nine mystery novels, **Rob Kantner** (www.Rob-Kantner.com) has published some four dozen suspense/crime stories and novellas, plus three nonfiction books and many articles and essays. His latest book is the collection *Trouble Is What I Do* (Point Blank, 2005). He lives with his wife Deanna on their rural Michigan horse farm.

Karen Harper on
The Tell-Tale Heart by Edgar Allan Poe (1846)

My education in mystery writing comes not only from years of reading suspense stories, but from teaching American and Brit Lit for seventeen years, both at the university and high school levels. No better way to learn something than to teach it. Though I've read hundreds of great mysteries, the classic writing which has most impacted both my historical mystery series and my contemporary suspense novels is that of the master, that inspiration for the yearly Mystery Writers of America awards, Edgar Allan Poe.

His poems and short stories may sound a bit melodramatic today, but how well the lessons he has to teach writers hold up over time. The novel format wasn't his thing, so I focus on one of his most seminal stories, "The Tell-Tale Heart."

"True! — nervous — very, very dreadfully nervous I had been and am," begins this work. If you don't recall this story, it involves an untrustworthy narrator (a madman) who obsesses about and then commits a murder but soon gives himself away during his statement to the police. I never had to read farther than this opening line to learn a few lessons from Poe: set the tone early, pull the reader into a point-of-view character, develop villains and torque up the tension as soon as possible. Above all, don't write a mystery with downtime: sunny skies and non-pressure prose. If your main characters are off-balance, if the hero/heroine is cold, sleepless, driven, dragged-out, that's exactly what you want.

Also, this tale — as well as other Poe works — occurs at night or at least in the dark. Crimes can certainly occur in the sunlight, but the effect of a walled-up room, a weird house or a stormy marsh still sets an eerie tone if presented in a fresh way. For my Queen Elizabeth I mystery series, I have used castles, towers and mazes. My suspense novels focus on unusual enclave settings such as unique small towns (with "a cast of creepy characters," said Publishers Weekly), an isolated Amish barn and an Everglades hunting camp. These may not be the House of Usher, but they are nonetheless inspired by Poe's details of dark lanterns, evil eyes and a beating heart buried under the floorboards.

The only thing I did not adopt from this work or others by Poe is his first-person point of view, but then short stories demand a more unified focus than novels. Having the murderer tell the tale works wonderfully for Poe since we experience the crime with the killer. Poe pulls us into the victim's fears without giving his point of view. The old man springs up from his bed, crying "Who's there?" He sits up, terrified to move but fearful of what the sounds could be, while all the time, he is being observed in the dark by the would-be killer. The old man gives a groan that arises from the bottom of the soul. This is Poe's reference in this story to what he elsewhere calls the dark night of the soul.

It is that fear of being trapped and endangered that I have learned from Poe to put into all my tales.

Karen Harper's *The Fatal Fashione* is book eight in The Queen Elizabeth I Mystery Series from St. Martin's. Her New

York Times and USA Today bestselling suspense novels include *The Falls, Dark Angel* and *Hurricane* (Mira). Her historical novels are *The Last Boleyn* and *Joan of Kent: Princess of Wales* (Random House).

Nancy Means Wright on
The Moonstone by Wilkie Collins (1868)

I remember it as a full moon, although it might have been a three-quarter. I was at our lake cottage in Vermont, and I'd just put the children to bed. Full of adrenaline from that luminous moon, I was wide awake with nothing to read. But wait — in the old, scarred bookcase, a copy of *The Moonstone*. I curled up with it on the sofa.

An ancient curse, a stained nightgown, Hindus lurking about an English manse, and, on the eve of Rachel Verinder's eighteenth birthday, a gift of the moonstone — a diamond the size of a plover's egg that "shone awfully out of the depths of its own brightness." A diamond that disappears that same night, sending owners, guests, and servants into a paroxysm of suspicion and fear — dashing the hopes of Franklin Blake, whose beloved Rachel has shut her door to him.

I was amazed by this 1868 novel whose Sergeant Cuff of Scotland Yard, our first English detective, uses methods of reconstructing a crime that still resonate in today's crime fiction. Cuff, whose face is "as sharp as a hatchet," his skin "as dry and withered as an autumn leaf." Whose steely eyes, encountering yours, look as if they expect "something more from you than you were aware of yourself."

But Sergeant Cuff relates only a small part of the story. There are multiple first person narrators. My favorite is the house steward, Gabriel Betteredge, a congenial 70ish man who often feels an "attack of detective fever" coming on. Like my own amateur sleuth, Ruth Willmarth, Betteredge is fiercely loyal, hospitable and pragmatic, imbued with the Puritan ethic of work as the salvation of the soul. He observes, he judges, he misjudges; he is often baffled and overwhelmed. And like my Ruth, who holds her own small prejudices and suspicions of strangers, he is often an unreliable narrator.

The narrators, trustworthy or fallible, provide not only suspense and drama, but humor as well. The evangelist Miss Clack with her ubiquitous tracts reappears in my own books (in part) as Ruth's self-righteous sister-in-law. For it was *The Moonstone* that led me to write in the personas of several characters in each of my books, hoping in this way to create, as Collins does, fully rounded — if flawed — individuals. "Right or wrong," as he states in his preface, the conduct of these characters "directs the course" of the novel's events.

For it was Collins' intent "to trace the influence of character on circumstance." It is the characters' quirks and desires, such as the passion of plain, misshapen Rosanna for Franklin, that shape the plot — to my mind, the best, the most organic way to write. Rosanna hides a vital clue down by the Shivering Sands; Rachel saw something traumatic the night of the diamond's disappearance, but will tell no one, not even Franklin, whom she loves. It is this maddening silence that gives the novel its main narrative drive.

There are myriad twists and turns in *The Moonstone*: a suicide, a little horror and violence, a generous helping of romance. The story weaves through the witnesses' spellbinding testimonies to its inevitable ending — which I won't divulge except to say that the lovers reunite, and order is restored. And isn't this why we write? To bring order back into our harried lives?

Yes. To close the book and sigh, the mystery resolved. And if the night is clear, to look out again at the faithful moon, and feel that, for a moment at least, all is right with the world.

Nancy Means Wright (www.nancymeanswright.com) has published eleven books, including five mystery novels with St. Martin's Press featuring earthy, hot-tempered dairy farmer Ruth Willmarth. *Mad Cow Nightmare* (2005) is the latest. A former Bread Loaf scholar and current scholar for Vermont Humanities Council, Nancy lives and writes in Cornwall, Vermont.

David Thurlo on
The Speckled Band by Arthur Conan Doyle (1892)

It wasn't easy being Sherlock Holmes in Shiprock, but for a while in 1959 *I* was the master sleuth. The Big Chief drive-in had just featured a *Hound of the Baskervilles* movie, and this Anglo boy was hooked. Somehow, I needed to experience more Holmes and Watson. Forget TV — we could only get two snowy channels — and it might be months before another Sherlock Holmes movie happened to come along.

There were no libraries in this corner of the Navajo Nation, at least during the summer. Comic books were often the only source of new non-adult reading material. I'd already consumed every book in the house — including a few I probably wasn't supposed to read.

At least Shiprock received monthly visits from a state library bookmobile. Guess who was first up the steps? I was already an old hand at this — I had a library card — the only ID a ten-year-old kid needed back then. I headed straight for Doyle in mystery fiction and selected a volume of short stories. There were at least a dozen Sherlock adventures between the covers. At one or two a day, I'd still have three weeks to read the other nine books I was going to select — now that my priorities had been met.

The first Sherlock Holmes story I chose to read was "The

Speckled Band." Maybe it was the title that drew me in, or the length — not too short, not too long. My British English, at ten, was rusty, and there were a lot of unfamiliar words to stumble across. Sure, I could find Waterloo Station on a map, but why would anyone have a sitting-room? This was Shiprock, in the desert, and even fog was foreign to me.

The story exceeded my wildest expectations. I'd always been interested in taking things apart, just to see how they worked, but with this tale I was messing with ideas. From the moment I began "The Speckled Band," it was a real challenge trying to keep up with Holmes, following his reasoning and logic and discovering whodunit. It was easy outguessing Dr. Watson, but Sherlock was a genius. As he often said, and as I began repeating to my friends, Holmes didn't just see, he *observed.* Each clue, no matter how insignificant it seemed, led to something important. I wished I could have been like Holmes.

With "The Speckled Band," I discovered how foreign Victorian England could be to a child in New Mexico. It wasn't just the climate. For example, I had a problem with what Holmes called the ventilator. My dad told me it wasn't some machine, it was just a wall vent. He pointed to the grill of our floor furnace, which allowed the passage of air. It made sense then.

Finally I got to something cool that I could relate to — the snake. Holmes and Watson had to deal with a "swamp adder," but we frequently encountered rattlesnakes in the desert. The critters would come into the yard at night hunting for mice, or curl up in the water box out back, waiting for us to discover them in the morning.

"The Speckled Band" was an amazing story, and I knew right then that if I ever wrote a mystery, I'd want to leave clues for the reader — challenging but not impossible to follow. After all, most of the fun in reading was putting yourself in the place of the hero. I continued my journey into Sherlock Holmes' world, seeing English villages, riding in traps and even wearing a deerstalker cap. I knew that someday I might even get to walk in real fog.

David Thurlo was raised on the Navajo Indian Nation, then left the Rez after high school to attend University of New Mexico. David and his wife Aimée are co-authors of the Ella Clah, Sister Agatha and Lee Nez mystery series. Their tenth Ella Clah mystery is *Mourning Dove* (2006).

Donna Andrews on
The Red Thumb Mark by R. Austin Freeman (1907)

I discovered R. Austin Freeman when *Masterpiece Theatre* broadcast *The Rivals of Sherlock Holmes*, including an episode featuring Freeman's sleuth, medical forensic specialist Dr. John Evelyn Thorndyke. When I learned it was based on a series of books, I did what any avid reader would do: started reading them.

I'd explored Hammett, Chandler, Christie, Sayers and other vintage mystery writers, but from the first chapter of *The Red Thumb Mark*, Freeman's Thorndyke books filled a need I hadn't yet articulated. They reopened a doorway into late Victorian London, where the great detective and his loyal sidekick solved mysteries through pure reason while sitting beside a roaring fire. Or took a hansom cab to the railway station to rescue some imperiled client. Or faced a deadly foe lurking in the tendrils of a London Particular.

The Red Thumb Mark begins, like Doyle's *A Study in Scarlet*, with the meeting of great detective and slower-witted chronicler. Though Thorndyke is not a consulting detective, he's both doctor and lawyer, and his "sphere of influence ... includes all cases in which a special knowledge of medicine or physical science can be brought to bear upon law." Or as I explained to people who'd never heard of him, a late Victorian Quincy, M.E.

Freeman was virtually unknown in the 1970s, when I spent many happy hours pursuing him through used bookstores. That was part of the appeal. I couldn't just visit the corner bookstore for a Freeman fix, so opening a new (to me) Freeman gave both the reader's thrill at finding another book by a well-loved author and the detective's triumph at successfully recapturing an elusive fugitive. And as a fledgling mystery reader, I learned an important lesson: the fare available in the chain stores was a small — and not necessarily the most interesting — part of what the genre offered.

Freeman is credited with inventing the inverted plot mystery, which shows first the crime and then the detective solving it. Inverted mysteries focus not on "who done it" but on "how can they possibly solve this?" (*Columbo* is the best-known modern example.) But *The Red Thumb Mark*, Thorndyke's first adventure, is a conventional narration. When I began to reread it before writing this, I found myself worrying: Would it hold up?

Yes, better than I expected. Freeman's not for everyone. Readers who demand a body in chapter one should look elsewhere, and the books sound formulaic if you read too many consecutively. But the formula's a solid one: a client with a seemingly impossible case throws himself at Thorndyke's mercy — in *The Red Thumb Mark*, it's Reuben Hornby, whose bloody fingerprint the police find at the crime scene. Thorndyke and his juniors gather data. Eventually Thorndyke becomes uncommunicative, and you know he'll soon produce the solution, hinging on some medical or scientific fact from his encyclopedic brain. Those who enjoy Holmes' witticisms at Watson's expense will appreciate Freeman's dry wit.

In short, readers who appreciate a vintage mystery's more

sedate pace and subtler charms will relish *The Red Thumb Mark* and the Thorndyke canon. And if, like me, you still begrudge Conan Doyle the time he spent on spiritualism and *The White Company* instead of Holmes, Freeman is a godsend.

As a writer, I think Freeman helped me make that critical leap from merely wanting more of a favorite author's work to taking up the pen and writing it myself. Freeman was clearly influenced by Doyle, and yet he also brought his very different skills and passions to the work, and expanded the scope of detective fiction. Reading him helped me realize that mystery was a not a settled empire, completely mapped and charted, but still a wilderness in which an aspiring writer might stake out a small territory of her own.

Donna Andrews (www.donnaandrews.com) is the author of the Meg Langslow series, most recently *No Nest for the Wicket* (St. Martin's, 2006), and the Turing Hopper series, most recently *Delete All Suspects* (Berkley, 2005). Her first mystery novel, *Murder With Puffins*, won St. Martin's 1997 Malice Domestic Award.

Michael Lister on
The Innocence of Father Brown by G.K. Chesterton (1911)

I wanted to write clerical detective mysteries before I knew anything about G.K. Chesterton or Father Brown. So when I happened upon the 1990 Avenel edition of *Father Brown Crime Stories* in a dusty old bookstore in Atlanta the year I graduated from college, it was nothing less than serendipitous. During that momentous year of transition, as I was being born into my adult life, Chesterton in many ways became my literary father and Brown the fictional father to my ecclesiastical sleuth, John Jordan.

It would be four years later, as I was finishing my graduate degree in theology and about to enter into full-time prison chaplaincy, that ex-cop turned prison chaplain, John Jordan, was born. But there's no doubt that the seeds of his birth had been planted in my discovery of Chesterton all those years earlier.

The birth of the clerical detective began late one night when, unable to find a good detective story while staying at the house of a boyhood friend, G.K. Chesterton decided to write his own. Of course, religion and murder go back a lot further than Chesterton's sleepless night — as far back as Cain and Abel in fact.

In Father Brown, Chesterton created an interesting and lovable character who has surprising insight into the darker side of humanity, a trait he attributed to hearing their darkest secrets in his confessional: "Has it never struck you that a man who does next to nothing but hear men's real sins is not likely to be wholly unaware of human evil?"

Like the plots of genre masters Conan Doyle and Agatha Christie, Chesterton's plots are enormously improbable. They shouldn't, however, be dismissed because of this. As Chesterton himself once wrote, they belong "to the grand and joyful company of the things called jokes. The story is a fancy; an avowedly fictitious fiction. We may say if we like that it is a very artificial form of art; I should prefer to say that it is professedly a toy, a thing that children 'pretend' with."

The irony of *The Innocence of Father Brown* is that Father Brown is not innocent at all. Or if he is, it is an innocence not of the mind but of the heart. Innocence does not imply ignorance nor does purity require naïveté. Because of his vocation, Father Brown, like all clerical detectives who have followed him, is in a unique position to understand humanity. As Ellis Peters, creator of Brother Cadfael, said, the approach of the religious detective "must rest mainly on the observation of character, which is of far more interest than forensic detail."

There are a number of ways John Jordan differs from Father Brown. Honor my father though I do, like any son I've had to find my own way. Besides I've had many literary fathers, and part of the fun of working in a genre is to play with and against its conventions. I owe as much to hardboiled writers like Hammett and Chandler as I do Chesterton. I knew from the very beginning that I would introduce a clerical detective into the world of the hardboiled detective novel, and I felt that prison chaplaincy was the place those two disparate worlds collide.

I think part of Father Brown's and Chaplain Jordan's appeal is their moral authority, but Brown and Jordan aren't merely out for justice. They're also ministers who see a crime scene as an opportunity to help those in need — they are not so much bloodhounds as hounds of heaven.

In just a few years, the ecclesiastical sleuth will celebrate its first century of crime-fighting and soul-saving. Thanks to the foundation Chesterton laid, the subgenre continues to thrive, and it doesn't take a prophet to foresee that commandments will continue to be broken and clerical cops will continue to patrol the celestial beat.

Michael Lister (www.MichaelLister.com) is the author of the acclaimed John Jordan mysteries, *Power in the Blood*, *Blood of the Lamb* and *The Body and the Blood*. Before becoming a full-time writer, Michael was the youngest chaplain within the Florida Department of Corrections. His seven years of prison chaplaincy bring authenticity and realism to his mysteries featuring ex-cop turned prison chaplain, John Jordan.

Betty Webb on
The Mysterious Affair at Styles by Agatha Christie (1920)

Back in the late '60s, while attending college in Los Angeles, I was a book snob. I would only read things considered "literary," e.g. works by John Updike, Aldous Huxley, Joan Didion, Doris Lessing and the like. I would just have soon gulped down a live goldfish as read a mystery.

Then I developed mononucleosis. I wasn't terribly sick, just sick enough that I couldn't summon the energy to attend class. Since I didn't have a television set (I was snobbish about TV, too), all I could do was lie on my daybed steeped in self-pity, wishing I'd either get well or just go ahead and die. After several weeks of this, a non-bookish friend of mine brought over a large carton of paperbacks he'd bought at a yard sale for five dollars. "I know you like books," he said. "There's about fifty of the things in there."

Too weak to sneer, I thanked him and went back to feeling sorry for myself. A few hours later, more out of boredom than anything else, I began rummaging through the carton, only to find it filled with mysteries, most of them by somebody named Agatha Christie. Disgusted, I went back to sleep.

The next day I blindly plucked a book out of the carton and leafed through it. *The Mysterious Affair at Styles* was set during World War I, which piqued my interest — history, you understand, was important. In it, some guy named Hastings was describing a murder that had been solved by a Belgian refugee friend of his named Hercule Poirot. Thinking that I might at least gain some insights on the Belgian refugee problem during the Great War, I began to read.

Three hours later I'd finished the book and was in a snit. Everything I'd always suspected about mysteries was true. The book was dumb and Agatha Christie was a cheat. She pretended she'd laid down all those clues, but of course she hadn't. I decided to write a letter, giving her a piece of my mind.

But first I had to make notes. I began reading again, double-checking to make certain I hadn't missed anything. To my horror, I discovered that yes, I'd missed all the clues she'd planted on pages 5, 6, 10, 11, 13 ... and just about every other page for the rest of the book. Slowly I began to realize that *Styles* was an intricate puzzle only an alert reader would solve. Shaken to the foundation of my snobbish being, I finally fell asleep dreaming of little men with fancy moustaches.

The next day I started working my way through the rest of the carton, pushing aside all the other mystery writers to concentrate on Agatha Christie. By the time I'd read every book in the box, my energy was back and I was ready for a trip to the library to check out every Christie I hadn't yet read. I wrote Christie a fan letter (which her secretary eventually answered). A month later I returned to school with a more open mind about mystery novels and the people who write them.

Did *The Mysterious Affair at Styles* cure my mononucleosis? Maybe, maybe not. But it did give me back the spirit I'd lost when I fell ill. The book also opened my eyes to the fact that not all brilliant authors write in the so-called literary tradition; some have other fish to fry. Today, my bookshelves contain approximately half mystery novels, half literary novels.

For the life of me, I still can't tell which are the most intelligent.

Betty Webb's (www.bettywebb-mystery.com) Lena Jones detective series — *Desert Shadows*, *Desert Wives* and *Desert Noir* — has garnered rave reviews from the New York Times, Chicago Tribune, Baltimore Sun and other national publications. *Desert Run* was released March 2006. She is also the Small Press reviewer at Mystery Scene Magazine.

Kerry Greenwood on
The Three Hostages by John Buchan (1924)

When someone invents a reliable time machine, just after I get back from the Library of Alexandria with my classical scholar and my skip (otherwise I might end up with the complete works of Menander and other duds), I shall invite John Buchan to stay at my house. His food shall be of the finest, infected with the best forms of bacteria, his seat shall be in the strongest draught and his sheets shall be definitively damp.

Why? Because this amazing man could only spare the time from being a lawyer, politician, historian, hill-walker, confidant of kings, etc., when he was sick. He looked on writing his "shockers" as pure convalescent hobby.

To a professional detective story writer, this is a sobering thought. For Buchan is the master of the form, understands it in a profound way and can write such exciting prose that by the end of some of his pages one can find oneself cheering. And he wasn't even trying... Sigh....

Take *The Three Hostages*. Only a man totally sure of himself would explain — in words of one syllable, in the first chapter — that the detective writer writes inductively and we read deductively, and that a good story can be made of three disparate clues, which the writer knows are connected but the reader does not. And then write the book based on just such a set of clues, a rhyme sent by an arrogant evildoer to the loved ones of the three stolen people.

"See?" says the magician. "The quickness of the hand deceives the eye..." and there out of his hat comes a most unexpected white rabbit with pink eyes.

Out of Buchan's hat comes a lovely cast of characters: the stolid Richard Hannay, the polymath Sandy Arbuthnot, Dr. Greenslade who walks 40 miles to remember his rhyme, masseuse Madame Breda, the sinister Dr. Newhover and the dreadful old woman who spins by the fire. And, best of all, the final confrontation of Mary Hannay and the villain, the horribly believable and most dangerous young man Medina.

The novel is notable for Buchan's belief in the strength and courage of women. No "shocker" writer of the time could have written such a female character. Mary remains a devoted wife and mother, and she has a steely integrity that Medina cannot counter. Hannay's complete trust in her planning and courage is touching and unique in the novels of the time. At one point he rushes off to consult with her to make sure that he does not "spoil her game." God bless him.

Buchan is not afraid to disappoint the reader for a reason. At the round-up of the bad guys, Medina is not touched. "We want," says Hannay, "success, not victory." Medina does not go down in a howling of public shame, though his organization is smashed beyond repair and his hostages are freed. It is Medina himself who insists on a final showdown with Hannay. Medina himself is his own downfall.

The achievements of *The Three Hostages* are multifold. It is an exemplar for anyone who wants to write a mystery. It is a primary feminist text for strong female characters. And it is, as Buchan would want me to say, a really, really good, strong, engrossing read.

Kerry Greenwood writes detective stories, historical novels, children's books and science fiction. She received the Lifetime Achievement Award from The Crime Writers of Australia and now wants another lifetime. She lives under firm feline management with two cats and a wizard. In her spare time she is a public defender for Victoria Legal Aid. In her spare, spare time she stares blankly out of the window.

Valerie Wolzien on
The Murder of Roger Ackroyd by Agatha Christie (1926)

In part, I became a writer of mystery novels because of a book I had yet to read: Agatha Christie's *The Murder of Roger Ackroyd*.

I grew up in a house lined with shelves stuffed with classic mystery novels. Yet, after a Nancy Drew binge in third grade, I didn't bother with mystery novels. I was, looking back, something of a literary snob. "Did Virginia Woolf read mysteries?" I might have asked if someone suggested I try reading an Agatha Christie novel. In fact, Virginia Woolf did, but I didn't — not yet.

Lying on the beach one summer during high school, surrounded by family members engrossed in fictional murder, I made what I thought was a clever suggestion — if I were to write a mystery, I announced, I would make the narrator the killer. "Been done," my father, probably irritated at my snobbish attitude toward his summer reading, told me. "You should read *The Murder of Roger Ackroyd*."

I wasn't into taking good advice at that particular point in my life. Determined to be a Serious Writer, I ignored mysteries and focused on that nebulous Great American Novel in the sky.

But I was never satisfied with any of my writing. Then, in my early twenties, I walked into a library in Green Bay, Wisconsin, and bumped, quite literally, into a display of Dame Agatha's work. Roger Ackroyd was an unusual name and one I remembered. I checked out the book, took it home, read it and became a convert. I loved the book, and I was sure I was capable of writing one just like it. I was completely wrong, of course, but the fact that I had thought of the same twist as was in one of the most famous mysteries ever written convinced me that mysteries were the genre for me.

I wrote and I read. I reread and I wrote. And, for the next few years I studied the classic mysteries I had despised earlier, returning over and over to the first mystery I had ever read.

In *The Murder of Roger Ackroyd*, I was impressed less by the narrator/murderer than by the characters and the way they related to each other and to the plot. Dr. Sheppard's sister, Caroline, is described as a woman with a "ferret-like curiosity and the staying power of a bloodhound." She is underestimated by the local — and incompetent — members of the police force. But her knowledge is unique and sought after by the ever clever Hercule Poirot.

Caroline Sheppard was the model for my first sleuth, Susan Henshaw. Initially, Susan is completely underestimated by the other characters in the book. She is endlessly curious, and she never gives up until she has discovered the identity of the killer. In *Murder at the PTA Luncheon*, the first book in my first series, Brett Fortesque, the officer in charge of discovering who killed the Vice President of the PTA, meets Susan and respects her knowledge much as Hercule Poirot did when he met Caroline Sheppard. Together they find the murderer. This combination has worked for the other thirteen books in the series.

But I've yet to write a mystery with a killer as the narrator.

Valerie Wolzien writes two mystery series. The first stars Susan Henshaw, housewife, mother and sleuth. The protagonist in her second series is Josie Pigeon, a young woman who owns her own contracting company as well as solving crimes. The most recent book in this series is *Death at a Premium*. Valerie lives with her family on the west bank of the Hudson River.

Ted Hertel, Jr. on
The Tower Treasure by Franklin W. Dixon (1927)

My family bought its first television in 1949. I sat enthralled in front of its glowing black and white eye for hours. *Howdy Doody* came on at 4:00 and I was hooked from the first day I saw it. So I was on that sofa for six years before the show that changed my life (some might say "wrecked it") came on: Walt Disney's *Mickey Mouse Club.*

I sat there watching Jimmie Dodd, Roy (the Big Mouseketeer), Cubby, Karen and, of course, Annette. But not even Annette hit me like *The Hardy Boys: The Mystery of the Applegate Treasure.* Here was a serial that ran for months. I *had* to know "just where are those gold doubloons and pieces of eight, pieces of eight, pieces of eight" that old man Applegate was hoarding. "I don't care if dinner's getting cold, Mom, I just *gotta* watch this!"

This was something totally new to me. Two young boys out solving crimes. Sure, their dad was Fenton Hardy, world famous detective. And there was the interfering Aunt Gertrude, as well. But Frank and Joe Hardy were only a bit older than I was *and they were having adventures* while I was sitting around on the couch, doing nothing. The credits told me that the story was based on a book. So I decided that I had to find and read that book.

My first stop (being the cheapskate that I was in those days … hmm, still am, too, I suppose) was the local library. I knew how to use the card catalog, so I could find any book I wanted. But my library was equally cheap, apparently, and it did not have the book. A small setback for this young book detective. I checked the school library (which had about forty books in it and no card catalog). Nothing. Of course, when I got older, I learned that many libraries simply did not carry "such trash," preferring that we read the classics, not recognizing that this book *was* a classic.

Then one fateful evening my parents dragged my brother, my sister and me to Gimbels Department Store to buy some clothes for the coming school year. *Bor*-ring. When that torture was finished, we three kids, set loose on our own, headed over to the book section. After a few minutes of looking, I discovered the Holy Grail: *The Tower Treasure* and *The House on the Cliff*, the first two Hardy Boys' books, *on sale* for 50 cents each!

I spent the next day reading the first book and the following day, the second. But there were more. I had seen them at Gimbels. I had the list on the dust jackets of the first two books. I had to have the rest of them. And eventually I did get them all, even when they cut them down in length and eliminated the dust jackets. I still have them to this day.

This set me on the path I was destined to follow. I began to write the adventures of "The Hertel Boys." Classics (though some might say "garbage") such as "The Silver Fox Mystery" rolled off the tip of my pen. (The typewriter was simply too much work.) Long before Lilian Jackson Braun thought of it, I was writing mysteries in which a cat (and a dog) solved crimes. My father's library card in hand, I went from the children's area of the library to the adult section, looking for Erle Stanley Gardner, Agatha Christie and Ellery Queen. Eventually I began writing in earnest: essays, short stories, a novel. Even my writers' group is called the Noirsketeers. None of this would ever have happened without Frank, Joe and Mickey.

That book of towering importance still holds a treasured place on the shelf of my library. I would not be where I am today without it.

Ted Hertel, Jr.'s first short story "My Bonnie Lies . . . " (*The Mammoth Book of Legal Thrillers*) was nominated for Macavity and Anthony Awards and received the Robert L. Fish Award. His short story "It's Crackers to Slip a Rozzer the Dropsey in Snide" (*Small Crimes*) was nominated for the Anthony.

Sharan Newman on
The Poet and the Lunatics by G.K. Chesterton (1929)

I first discovered the works of G.K. Chesterton when I was sixteen. I knew nothing about him; I was only intrigued by the title of the book on the library shelf, *The Poet and the Lunatics*. Like most literary sixteen-year-olds, I suspected that I might be both.

The hero of these loosely-connected tales is Gabriel Gale, a tall, blond, angular artist and poet. He happens upon situations where a crime has either occurred or is about to. Sometimes he is called in by his friend Dr. Garth. Very often Gale is laughed at when he proposes his solution, for he sees the world very differently from those around him. He follows derailed trains of thought to their illogical crashing point by, as he modestly explains, thinking like a lunatic.

You can see how this would appeal to an adolescent.

Gale's pronouncements were equally attractive. When one character comments on the "eccentricities of genius," Gale responds:

"Genius ought to be centric. It ought to be at the core of the cosmos, not on the revolving edges. People seem to think it a compliment to accuse one of being an outsider, and to talk about the eccentricities of genius. What would they think, if I said I only wish to God I had the centricities of genius?"

"They'd think it was the beer," replied Dr. Garth.

"The Fantastic Friends"

But while finding a soul mate in this misunderstood poet, I was also absorbing the richness of Chesterton's prose. He was a poet and an artist himself, although much more portly than his protagonist. His descriptions are full of Anglo-Saxon alliteration and painterly images.

"Sir Owen was a little restless man, with a large head, a bristly grey moustache and a grey fan of hair like the crest of a cockatoo." ("The Shadow of the Shark")

More than wordplay, Chesterton used these descriptions to set the mood of his stories and to foreshadow the conclusion of the story.

Madness is the theme in these stories, and the fine line we walk between eccentricity and insanity. A man who frees a caged tropical bird into an English winter may be odd and misguided, but sane. A man who liberates fish from water into the deadly air has crossed the threshold of madness.

At that point in my life when one is neither child nor adult and seems to have little control over anything, these stories had a great impact. I loved the writing and the character of Gabriel Gale. I read this and other Chesterton collections over and over.

I now know that Chesterton was a devout Catholic, but I didn't notice it in my first reading and, even now, I don't see any doctrine in his work. Gabriel Gale's God feels like that of the Transcendentalists, more of a wise creator of nature than anything to do with Judeo-Christian tradition.

What Chesterton seems concerned with in these stories is limits. The form of insanity that he deals with most often is megalomania. But I see the characters as people who simply can't find any structure in their lives. They have lost all sense of proportion and can't tell the difference between stepping off a curb and jumping off a precipice. As a writer, this is a tremendously important lesson, one which I haven't fully learned. Stories need shape, edges, texture and resolution. It's fun to follow up any fancy one has, but if it's in a story, it has to have something to do with the plot.

Looking askew at the world makes it not only more interesting, but also more amusing. Gale often reflects on life in passing, sometimes while standing on his head. He knows that his particular form of insanity is a luxury. "Again Gale had to remind himself that even poets can only go mad on condition that a good many people connected with them stay sane...."

Chesterton and I both appreciated the madness and the limits.

Sharan Newman is the author of the award-winning Catherine Levendeur mystery series set in medieval France. The latest of these is *The Witch in the Well* for which she received the Bruce Alexander Award for best historical mystery. As a medieval historian and frequent traveler to France, she has also written *The Real History Behind the Da Vinci Code*.

Jan Burke on
Red Harvest by Dashiell Hammett (1929)

"Are you married?"
"Don't start that."
"Then you are?"
"No."
"I'll bet your wife's glad of it."
I was trying to find a suitable come-back for that wise-crack when a distant light gleamed up the road.

The above is taken from Dashiell Hammett's *Red Harvest*. The person trying to find the suitable comeback is the Continental Op, the unnamed protagonist of two novels and many short stories.

The woman — perhaps the only person to ever leave the Op hunting for a snappy retort — is the irresistible Dinah Brand, an unabashedly greedy hustler. Here's part of the Op's first description of her:

Her face was the face of a girl of twenty-five already showing signs of wear.... Her coarse hair — brown — needed trimming and was parted crookedly. One side of her upper lip had been rouged higher than the other. Her dress was of a particularly unbecoming wine color, and it gaped here and there down one side, where she had neglected to snap the fasteners or they had popped open. There was a run down the front of her left stocking.

This was the Dinah Brand who took her pick of Poisonville's men, according to what I had been told.

Later, when the Op and Dinah drink and dine together at her place, the Op tells us: "She wasn't a very good cook, but we ate as if she were."

Dinah Brand, you see, has a way of making you enjoy your appetite, whatever may be on your plate. I think I fell in love with this book because of her. One of the strongest female characters ever to grace the pages of detective fiction, she never appears completely put together — her stockings are worn crooked or have runs, her dresses don't fit quite right, her house is cluttered. She's believably full of contradictions. She's also more full of life than anyone else in Personville, and the role she plays in both its downfall and redemption is unforgettable.

Published in 1929, Hammett's remarkable debut novel has a great deal to recommend it. The Op's contemporaries in detective fiction were often priggish intellectuals who coolly resolved filthy little matters like murder from above the fray. The Op not only enters the fray, he turns up the heat. His hands get dirty. More importantly, he does not emerge unaffected.

The story of a tough but honest man set among warring gangs in a corrupt mining town could have easily become a cut-rate cowboy story. Instead, Hammett gave us a lean and finely crafted thriller. The dialogue snaps, and the story is sharp-edged, gritty and full of action. But like the heavy-set Op, it carries more on its frame than the average hard-boiled tale. *Red*

Harvest explores the effects of violence on all concerned, and not as an intellectual exercise. The reader feels the result of that exploration bone-deep. One closes the book feeling as if the Earth has doubled its gravity.

Because I had read *Red Harvest*, I learned that crime fiction could be more than diversion — as valuable as diversion may be when you want it. I don't know if my interest in mystery novels would have continued if I hadn't come across this book when I was in my twenties.

By the time I began my own first novel, that influence meant that I wanted to write books in which violence changed those who encountered it, in which murder would be more than a logic problem.

Rereading the book both daunted and inspired me while I worked on *Goodnight, Irene*. One must accept that he or she will never come close to Hammett, and write anyway. Like Dinah Brand, imperfect but gamely fighting. I remain grateful to Hammett for all there is to learn from *Red Harvest*.

Jan Burke is the author of ten novels and a collection of short stories. Her novels include *Bloodlines*, *Nine* and *Bones*, which won the Edgar®. *Imperfect* will be published by Simon & Schuster in 2006. She is the founder of the Crime Lab Project and a member of the board of the California Forensic Science Institute.

Dean James on
Mystery Mile by Margery Allingham (1930)

Nancy Drew started me on my life of crime. Like so many writers of my generation, once I discovered the juvenile series detectives, I was hooked. From Nancy Drew I went on to discover Judy Bolton and the Dana Girls, the Hardy Boys and

Ken Holt. Not to mention Trixie Belden and the Three Investigators.

The wonderful adventures in these books thrilled a farm boy from Mississippi and opened up a world of possibilities. I devoured stories of romance and adventure, moving on to Victoria Holt and Mary Stewart and Phyllis A. Whitney ... the list is practically endless.

And then I discovered Margery Allingham. I was in graduate school by this time, and my escape from the rigors of academia came in the form of used paperback mysteries. I bought an omnibus of Allingham's first three Campion novels. The first book, *The Crime at Black Dudley*, was amusing, but when I started the second one, *Mystery Mile*, I began to get a sense that I was on to something truly special.

Mystery Mile is a romantic adventure tale, not unlike an adult version of one of the classic Nancy Drew or Hardy Boys scenarios, replete with spooky houses and sinister criminals. Albert Campion, now firmly a hero, is mild and unassuming on the surface, sharp and deadly beneath the facade. By turns urbane and witty, then brisk and decisive, he offers just about everything one could ask of a series character.

Margery Allingham went on to write better, more complex, more emotionally rich stories, like her classic *The Tiger in the Smoke*, but *Mystery Mile* remains a sentimental favorite. This particular book embodies Allingham's wonderful sense of fun, her quirky humor, and her sheer zest in a way that made all her work highly individual, even when she turned more serious.

The mysteries I love best, and the ones to which I turn for inspiration, are the ones that combine richness of character with a distinctive sense of humor. No matter what I write, I think my own sense of humor comes through, and this is nowhere more evident than in the Simon Kirby-Jones mysteries. These books are intended to be flat-out fun, and most readers have responded to them in that way.

Lately I've been working in a somewhat different vein, moving more toward a mixture of the serious with the comic, just as Allingham did. As Jimmie Ruth Evans, I am telling the stories of characters more down-to-earth and more "real," in a sense, than I've written about before. Always there before me, as the perfect combination of character, humor, plot and atmosphere, is Margery Allingham. She is the epitome I will always strive to reach.

Dean James is Manager of Murder by the Book in Houston, one of the nation's oldest and largest mystery bookstores. He is the author of eight mystery novels, including *Baked to Death* (Kensington, 2005), and, writing as Jimmie Ruth Evans, *Flamingo Fatale* (Berkley Prime Crime, 2005).

Katherine Hall Page on
Murder at the Vicarage by Agatha Christie (1930)

Murder at the Vicarage is one of the first mysteries I read. For me, Jane Marple was — and remains — the quintessential female sleuth, relying on her own keen powers of observation and intuition as the basic tools for detection. She and Dame Agatha would scorn the current use of the Internet to ferret out information, having no need for Google. Instead, Miss Marple displays an uncanny ability to make connections between apparently disparate individuals and events, past and present. Human beings are much of a type, as are the situations in which they find themselves.

Agatha Christie set the bar. As I write, it's one I gaze upon from below with admiration, longing and, very occasionally, a glimmer of recognition. The classic village mystery, of which *Murder at the Vicarage* may be the best example, is the genre into which my own Faith Fairchild series falls. However, like

Agatha Christie, I do not limit the locale to places like St. Mary Mead or in my case, Aleford, Massachusetts, but broaden the definition to include New York City, France, Maine, Vermont and Norway. What motivates individuals to commit murder knows no borders. The kinds of communication that exist in a village exist in a city, a country. Miss Marple with her bird watching binoculars or sudden need to weed her garden becomes transformed into someone looking into apartment windows across an airshaft or the individual who stuffs newspapers into a trash bag heading for the curb to see who's moving in.

It all comes down to a passionate interest in people. Griselda Clement, the vicar's wife, describes Miss Marple as "the worst cat in the village...she always knows every single thing that happens — and draws the worst inferences from it." Much as I like Griselda, I find this a bit harsh. In *The Body in the Library*, Jane's friend, Dolly Bantry says, "People call her a scandal-monger, but she isn't really. Jane Marple's really a remarkable woman." Faith and I would concur, sharing a penchant for Miss Marple's self-described "hobby" of "studying people, human nature if you will." I think of my sleuth as someone who metaphorically takes a stick and pokes beneath the surface of a pond to find out what's underneath, someone who wants to know what's behind an individual's public face and explore any disparities.

Another reason that *Murder at the Vicarage* has had such a strong influence on my writing has to do with the actress, Margaret Rutherford, who played Jane Marple in four films: *Murder She Said, Murder at the Gallop, Murder Most Foul* and *Murder Ahoy* (1961 to 1964). Margaret Rutherford was Jane Marple for me, and still is despite the valiant efforts of PBS. The Rutherford movies combined elements of humor with elements of suspense, which is my goal. Agatha Christie was not happy with the choice of the actress, quite unlike tall, slim, Jane Marple of the "china-blue" eyes. Christie said of Rutherford,

"To me, she's always looked like a bloodhound." Eventually the author was pleased with the casting and dedicated *The Mirror Crack'd from Side to Side* (1962) to "My good friend, Margaret Rutherford."

Although it was not something I consciously realized until after my first book was published, there are many similarities between clerical wives Griselda and Faith. Faith, like Griselda, chafes at the fishbowl existence of parish life and both represent an outsider's perspective — in Faith's case, a native of the Big Apple finding herself in New England's more bucolic orchards.

I have not written about the plot of *Murder at the Vicarage*. I hope that you will now read or reread it immediately upon closing this book. There are a plethora of plausible suspects, plenty of red herrings, a thoroughly unpleasant victim — always satisfying — and above all, one of the finest creations in mystery fiction, Miss Jane Marple. As the vicar himself says, "There is no detective in England equal to a spinster lady of uncertain age with plenty of time on her hands."

Katherine Hall Page, guest of honor at Malice Domestic XVIII, writes an Agatha Award-winning series featuring amateur sleuth/caterer Faith Fairchild. *The Body in the Ivy* (Morrow, 2006) is Page's latest, along with a young adult novel, *Club Meds* (Simon and Schuster, 2006). She lives in Massachusetts with her husband and son.

Aaron Elkins on
The Complete Sherlock Holmes by Arthur Conan Doyle (1930)

The walls of my office are covered with photos of the fine mystery writers that I've had the good fortune to meet and know as a result of being one of the fraternity myself. Many have become good friends. Elizabeth Peters, Earl Emerson, Donald Westlake, Sue Grafton, Dorothy Cannell, Bill Pronzini, Marcia Muller, Loren Estleman, Evan Hunter, Sarah Caudwell, Lawrence Block, Mary Higgins Clark — but in pride of place, all by itself in the center, is a huge black-and-white photograph (two feet by three) of a man's face in profile. He is the only person there that I've never met, but I know him best of all. He wears a deerstalker hat, he is smoking a curved pipe, and his noble nose is perhaps three inches from the huge magnifying glass he holds in his hand.

He is, of course, Sherlock Holmes, or rather Basil Rathbone, the Sherlock Holmes of my childhood and therefore, *the* Sherlock Holmes, despite the paper-thin plots of those old movies and the brilliantly idiosyncratic portrayal of Jeremy Brett fifty years later.

Doubleday's edition of *The Complete Sherlock Holmes* was the first adult book I ever owned, given to me for my eleventh birthday at a time when my recreational reading consisted of juvenile-edition adventure stories — Robin Hood, King Arthur, Tarzan — and sports stories. It was a pretty disappointing gift (not to say intimidating, at 1,122 pages), and so it was a good two years before I got around to taking a crack at it. The moment I opened it and read that first line by "Dr. John H. Watson, M.D., late of the Army Medical Department," I was hooked: "In the year 1878 I took my degree of Doctor of Medicine of the University of London..." There was something about the simple elegance of the words that immediately brought me, like so many millions of others, to the echoing, fog-shrouded streets of Victorian London, and I read the whole 158 pages of *A Study in Scarlet* in a single sitting, surely a record for me.

I was, as we might say now, blown away. The plotting, the wit, the beauty of the words all charmed me, and the rest of the book went equally fast. When it was done, I went right back to the beginning and started again. And again. It was probably somewhere about the third reading that I realized that one of the things that so enchanted me was the fact that the center of every one of these wonderful stories wasn't the passion, or bravery, or violent action that I was used to — it was *intellect*. These were *detective* stories in the truest sense of the word. And I loved them.

Over 30 years later, when I tried my own hand at detective fiction, it was Arthur Conan Doyle that was my inspiration. Oh, by then I had read the exploits of a good many other "intellectual" or "scientific" detective heroes — R. Austin Freeman's Dr. Thorndyke, and G.K. Chesterton's Father Brown, and of course Agatha Christie's little man of the little gray cells, Hercule Poirot. I had enjoyed them all, but Sherlock Holmes towered over all of them. He was my model, and I mean that literally. He still is.

When my first book, *Fellowship of Fear*, was published, it got a good many satisfying reviews, but best of all by a country mile was the Houston Post's exuberant "Whee! A new Sherlock Holmes rises before us!"

That's up on my wall too, the only review in over twenty years of reviews, that's there.

Aaron Elkins' twenty novels have garnered an Edgar, an Agatha (with his wife Charlotte) and a Nero Wolfe Award. His books have been selections of the major book clubs, have been made into a major ABC television series and have been published in a dozen languages.

Michael A. Black on
The Maltese Falcon by Dashiell Hammett (1930)

The Maltese Falcon is generally regarded as Dashiell Hammett's greatest work. It holds the distinction of having been made into three film versions, one of which was directed by John Huston and starred Humphrey Bogart. It was the role that made Bogie's career, although it had originally been offered to the reigning tough-guy actor of the times, George Raft. The first two film versions, only one of which used the novel's actual title, didn't capture the quintessential toughness of the novel. This was where Huston succeeded, and he did so by merely transferring Hammett's book to the screen, scene for scene, and leaving the dialogue basically untouched.

I saw the movie on late-night TV long before I picked up the novel. And when I did, I was amazed to read that the description of Sam Spade was almost reminiscent of Bogart: "He looked rather like a blond satan." But moreover, I became enamored with the laconic, understated style. Hammett knew the importance of minimalism in establishing setting. Take, for instance, the description of Spade's office in that first scene: "The tappity-tap and the thin bell and muffled whir of Effie Perine's typing came through the closed door ... Ragged grey flakes of cigarette ash dotted the yellow top of the desk ... The ashes on the desk twitched and crawled in the current." The man could write.

Hammett was largely self-taught. His interesting life gave him a unique vantage point from which to write about crime and the people close to it. As his contemporary, Raymond Chandler once said, "[Hammett] took murder out of the boardroom and put it back in the alley where it belonged." Hammett spent the years following World War I as a Pinkerton Detective. In the early days of the twentieth century, the Pinkertons were far more than just ordinary private dicks. Many times, they were sent to lawless areas, such as the boom towns of Montana, where Hammett was the closest thing to the law available. He used these experiences in his writing.

For me, what Hammett accomplished with his short, staccato sentences and unrelenting pacing set a standard of excellence that I've always sought to emulate. Many people look at the hardboiled school — and the pulp writers in particular — as purveyors of gratuitous violence. But this is not the case with Hammett. In fact, in *The Maltese Falcon*, none of the murders happen on-stage, yet the sense of foreboding menace is both implicit and intrinsic. This is what sets Hammett apart from the other writers of his era. He's able to tiptoe through a violent story with a grace and elegance that are not readily apparent as tough-guy Sam Spade smacks people around and forces "dames" to strip in front of him.

Hammett also captured the moral ambiguity of the hardboiled anti-hero. Long before movie audiences would be thrilling to the portrayals of such iconoclastic movie actors as Steve McQueen or Russell Crowe, Hammett's Sam Spade pushed the boundaries of convention. No longer a white knight upon a stallion, Hammett introduced men who slunk through the urban jungles with a will to survive and prosper, but still with an underlying code that ultimately forced them to do the right thing. Thus Spade, who had been sleeping with the wife of his partner, Miles Archer, long before the man ended up dead, still knows that "when a man's partner is murdered, you have to do something about it." So it's inevitable that he has to turn over the woman he loves to the cops, when he realizes she was the one who pulled the trigger.

The Maltese Falcon was written sparingly, in a point of view that can best be termed third-person limited. The reader does not get much of Spade's internal musings, but as readers we don't need them. We're just along for the ride. It's the stuff that dreams are made of.

Chicago-area police officer **Michael A. Black** is the author of the acclaimed Ron Shade series, including *A Killing Frost*, *Windy City Knights* and *A Final Judgment*. Mike's standalone thrillers, *The Heist*, and his newest, *Freeze Me, Tender*, are out in bookstores now. He's currently working on a technothriller entitled *Blood Trails*.

Kate Flora on
Strong Poison by Dorothy L. Sayers (1930)

I belong to the Nancy Drew generation, inspired by child-hood reading and late '60s/early '70s feminism to explore how women could be the heroes of their own adventures. I wanted to write books where the protagonist saved herself, where family ties and relationships had an acknowledged effect on the main character's life, and where women had to deal with conflict and danger, and — perhaps most radical of all — their own sexuality. For much of what I wanted to explore, though, Nancy wasn't the right role model. Luckily, I found a hero in Dorothy Sayers' *Strong Poison*.

From the dramatic opening line, "There were crimson roses on the bench; they looked like splashes of blood," this mystery plunges directly into the judge's summary at mystery writer Harriet Vane's trial for the murder, by arsenic, of her former lover. Philip Boyes, we are told, represented himself as being conscientiously opposed to any formal marriage. Harriet Vane, worn out from his "unceasing importunities," finally consented to live "on terms of intimacy with him, outside the bonds of marriage." After a year of this arrangement, the couple quarreled and separated. The reason? Boyes had proposed marriage.

How exciting, as a reader and writer seeking role models, to come upon this character. Harriet Vane was a woman of such strong character that when Boyes proposed marriage, she wasn't grateful, she was outraged that, after persuading her against her will to accept his principles of conduct, he then renounced those principles himself. Harriet Vane "didn't like having matrimony offered as a bad-conduct prize." Much to

Mr. Boyes' shock and chagrin, she promptly ended the relationship.

When the jury fails to agree, Lord Peter Wimsey, who, during the trial has become attracted to Miss Vane, proposes to investigate on her behalf. When he visits her in prison, their conversation becomes the second delight of the book — a smart man and woman both holding their own in a witty dialogue.

Vane: "I thought Philip had made both himself and me ridiculous, and the minute I saw that — well, the whole thing simply shut down — flop!"

Wimsey: "I quite see that. Such a Victorian attitude, too, for a man with advanced ideas. He for God only, she for God in him, and so on. Well I'm glad you feel like that about it."

Vane: "Are you? It's not going to be exactly helpful in the present crisis."

Wimsey: "No; I was looking beyond that. What I mean to say is, when all this over, I want to marry you, if you can put up with me and all that."

She frowns, revealing that this proposal is her 47th. Later, somewhat mollified, she asks, "But, by the way, you're bearing in mind, aren't you, that I've had a lover?"

"Oh, yes. So have I, if it comes to that. In fact, several. It's the sort of thing that might happen to anybody. I can produce quite good testimonials. I'm told I make love rather nicely."

Wimsey's response shows such frankness and broadness of mind I yelled "Eureka!" Here were men and women being allowed to be both entertaining and honest.

Harriet Vane is discharged without a stain upon her character, freed by Wimsey's sleuthing. There are golden chrysanthemums on the judge's bench that "looked like burning banners." Carrying those burning banners, I have created Thea Kozak, my intelligent and forthright young sleuth, inspired by Sayers to allow Thea to have relationships that are mentally, emotionally, and physically honest and strong.

Kate Flora (www.kateflora.com.) is the author of six Thea Kozak mysteries and *Finding Amy*, the true story of a murder in Maine, and, as Katharine Clark, the suspense novel, *Steal Away*. Flora teaches writing for Grub Street in Boston. She is a past president of Sisters in Crime and a partner in Level Best Books. Flora is pursuing an MFA in creative writing at Vermont College.

Mark Richard Zubro on
Freddy the Detective by Walter R. Brooks (1932)

I imagine that many editors of volumes such as this are looking for serious articles on weighty subjects. Something along the lines of "The Oresti and Aeschylus: Mystery in Ancient Greek Tragedies and How They Changed My Life." Or at the very least "My Love Affair with Agatha Christie: How My World Changed Because of Her Brilliance." Well, sorry. I'm not trying to be funny or trivialize the subject of mysteries or what influenced me into developing my life long love for them, or what got me interested in writing them.

Although, after reading *The Murder of Roger Ackroyd* in my early teens, I didn't read another of Agatha's mysteries for 30 years. I'm still not sure I've forgiven her for that ending, but after all these years, I've come to appreciate what a brilliant plotter she was.

We mystery people are serious about our genre, and we should be. I once heard Sandra Brown at a convention give a speech on her writing, done mostly in the romance genre. To paraphrase: Sandra said that she was serious when she sat down to write, that her editor was serious when her books were being edited, the company was serious when they sent her a check, and the bank was certainly serious when Sandra took that check to the bank to cash it.

All this is preface to the fact that the book that influenced me the most in my writing life is a children's book. The one above all the others that got me started was *Freddy the Detective* by Walter R. Brooks. I must have read it when I was in the third or fourth grade, certainly no later than that. The book was one of a series of children's book in which Freddy, a pig, and his barnyard companions had a succession of adventures.

In *Freddy the Detective,* Freddy had read some of Sherlock Holmes' adventures, and he was teaching himself how to be a detective, look for clues and be logical. As Freddy's expertise grew and as he solved cases, other animals became interested. Eventually, he went into business with Mrs. Wiggins, the cow. They were perfect partners. As the book says, "It was an excellent combination, he supplying the ideas and she the common sense, neither of which is of much use without the other." This made eminent sense to me then and now.

More, in terms of detection, Freddy proves through the use of what we would call forensic evidence that his friend Jinx, the cat, did not commit a horrible crime.

So Freddy's world was one of ideas, logic and common sense, all based on provable evidence. At the heart of this series were the bonds of friendship, the triumph of bravery, endurance, and the importance of having a clear eye for doing what was right and what needed to be done. That was the kind of world that appealed to me then and still does today. Better these values than the notion of some Cosmic Superhero who has this vast series of galactic ledgers keeping track of us in some Santa Clausian way.

Further, Freddy was reading Sherlock Holmes. If Freddy could read Sherlock Holmes, I figured, then I could read Sherlock Holmes. In the series of books, Freddy was also a writer. What more lethal combination for a child? A hero who reads and writes. That year I asked for Holmes stories for Christmas. I got them. I loved them. Thank you, Freddy the pig.

Mark Richard Zubro has written eighteen mysteries. His latest is *Everyone's Dead But Us* from St. Martin's Press. Mark retired in June 2006 after 34 years of teaching and twenty years as president of his teachers' union. In retirement, he plans to write, read, eat chocolate and nap.

Margaret Maron on
Have His Carcase by Dorothy L. Sayers (1932)

My mother was an avid mystery reader and when I finished my own monthly supply of "age-appropriate" library books, I would sneak hers. Her tastes ran mainly to softboiled series: Leslie Ford's Grace Latham/Colonel Primrose, Erle Stanley Gardner's Perry Mason, Agatha Christie's Miss Marple and Hercule Poirot. My vision of life in Manhattan was shaped by the sophisticated chatter of Frances and Richard Lockridge's Mr. and Mrs. North and Dashiell Hammet's Nick and Nora Charles — all amusing, all diverting, all so interchangeable that I never noticed whether I was reading the third or the thirteenth of the series.

I'm sure I must have read a Lord Peter Wimsey novel before I picked up *Have His Carcase* when I was around fourteen or fifteen, because his name was certainly familiar to me. This book began with a Harriet Vane on a walking trip along the southwest coast of England. Lord Peter was mentioned in the third sentence, but it was a Lord Peter who had evidently met and proposed to this Harriet Vane in an earlier book. Also in that third sentence was the statement that she had been tried and acquitted of murder.

Huh?

Series characters had histories that affected the story line of the books that followed?

The Norths and the Charleses never got past the cocktail

hour; Jane Marple and Hercule Poirot stayed the same till the very end, when Christie put him in a nursing home for his final adventure; and Perry Mason never really kissed Della Street, much less bedded her. But in *Have His Carcase*, Harriet Vane becomes a full-fledged detective in her own right and it is made abundantly clear that the romance will deepen between them. It immediately sent me scrambling for *Strong Poison* so that I could read the whole backstory, and it made me seek out all the Sayers books written after it. Although only *Gaudy Night* and *Busman's Honeymoon* put Harriet Vane at the center, I was delighted to see sly hints dropped in the intervening books that she was still in Lord Peter's life.

The murder mystery in *Have His Carcase* is one of those intricate and complicated plots so dear to the hearts of Golden Age readers — full of timetables, dubious clues, esoteric bits of arcane knowledge, and some of the most improbable logic any writer could cram into a single book. At fifteen, I closed it with enormous satisfaction. At 35, when I reread it while plotting my own first novel, I kept thinking, "Why the devil didn't the killer simply waylay the victim on a dark and stormy night? If he was going to bring in two accomplices, why not just have them swear they were having drinks together in a crowded smoke-filled London pub instead of concocting an elaborate charade that was bound to cause suspicion?"

Although none of my plots will ever depend on split-second timing or on knowing Romanov history or the proper care of a straight razor, *Have His Carcase* did inspire me to create series characters who age and change in a linear progression from one book to the next. It made me write the kind of book I still like to read.

Margaret Maron's *Bootlegger's Daughter* is among the 100 Favorite Mysteries of the Century as selected by the Independent Mystery Booksellers Association. In 2004, *Last Lessons of*

Summer won the North Carolina Literary and Historical Association's Sir Walter Raleigh Award. Her latest novel is *Winter's Child* (2006).

P.M. Carlson on
The Fear Sign aka Sweet Danger by Margery Allingham (1933)

Writers don't write alone. As we pull places and characters and events from the murky swirl of our not-yet-thoughts, ghosts hover — wisps of people we've met, stories we've read, situations we want to challenge. When I began writing mysteries, I wanted to show that a woman could care about family and career and still have adventures. A couple of insistent ghosts showed up from Margery Allingham's *The Fear Sign*, one of the earlier Albert Campion mysteries. One was Campion, of course, bright and brave enough to play the role of the very proper Hereditary Paladin of Averna early in *The Fear Sign*, but more often hiding from enemies and even friends behind a clownish facade of pranks and inane speech. In *The Fear Sign* a wealthy villain tried to stop Campion's meddling by hiring him to go abroad. This "personage" explained the detailed preparations, ending:

"*Your usual tailor has supplied a complete tropical outfit, which is waiting for you on board the Marquisita.*"

"*Splendid! Now all I've got to think about is a bottle of Mothersill, and a bag of nuts for the natives, I suppose.*"

"*That facetiousness,*" *said the personage.* "*I've heard about that. I find it very irritating myself.*"

For me *The Fear Sign* stood out even from other Campion mysteries because it introduced young Amanda Fitton. She supported her impoverished family by running a mill and by trying to make the threadbare family home into an appealing inn. Only seventeen, Amanda was both scientist and mechanic. She ran a dynamo to recharge people's wireless batteries and restored an ancient automobile to running order. Like a youthful Rosie the Riveter, the capable Amanda showed us that women could run a business or a country (or a war — in later books, the grown-up Amanda designed airplanes). Unlike previous Allingham heroines who were caring and courageous but basically reactive, Amanda made things happen.

She could even deal with Campion. The "personage" quoted above found Campion's foolish prattle irritating. Compare Amanda's reaction as she showed him around her place, commenting:

"Appearances matter an awful lot."

"Oh, rather," said Mr. Campion. "I knew a man once who carried it to excess, though. His name was Gosling, you see, so he always dressed in grey and yellow, and occasionally wore a great false beak.... And finally he moved into a wooden house with just slats in front instead of windows, and you opened the front door with a pulley on the roof. It had a natty little letterbox on the front gate with 'The Coop' painted on it. Soon after, his wife left him and the Borough Council stepped in. But I see you don't believe me."

"Oh, but I do," said Amanda. "I was his wife. Come and see the mill."

She enjoyed his inanities, but not just as audience — as participant too. It was a tiny moment in the book, but a signal that these two understood each other and could trust each other as teammates when the danger increased.

My mysteries are American, and I don't write about lost earldoms. But I too love science, and family, and theatre, and the joy of shared adventures. My characters juggle these often competing values as they solve crimes: statistician Maggie Ryan and actor Nick O'Connor build a family, Deputy Sheriff Marty Hopkins struggles to reconcile her role as mother with her role as law enforcement officer, and Bridget Mooney is driven by family duty as well as love for the stage. For me, the playful spirits of Albert and Amanda still inspire.

P.M. Carlson taught psychology and statistics at Cornell University before turning to mysteries. Her novels have been nominated for the Edgar, Macavity and Anthony Awards, and one made the Drood Review's Editors' Choice List. A former President of Sisters in Crime, she lived several years in southern Indiana, the setting of *Deathwind*, a Deputy Sheriff Marty Hopkins novel.

Elaine Viets on
The Sign of the Twisted Candles by Carolyn Keene (1933)

When I was nine, my mother gave me her Nancy Drew mysteries from the 1930s. She thought they were sweet, safe books. I thought they were like handing a bomb to an anarchist. They blew apart my ordinary life in Florissant, Missouri.

Parents never understood that Nancy was subversive. She had everything we wanted. Her cool dad bought her a car. Her mother was delightfully and distantly dead. She never said, "You're not going out in that getup, young lady!" Instead, Nancy had a motherly housekeeper who gave her good meals, good advice and no criticism. Her boyfriend, Ned Nickerson, was there when she wanted him, but never tried to guilt her into giving it up on the family room couch.

Nancy and her "chums" were exotic. They used words like "quaint" and "ruse." A dinner started with "jellied consomme" and ended with "nut bread, ice cream, chocolate layer cake."

I had no idea what jellied consommé was, but I knew it wasn't served in Florissant. Chums who ate three desserts knew how to live.

While I was in college, Nancy Drew disappeared from my bookshelf. I forgot about the titian-haired sleuth — or thought I did. Years later, after I'd written my ninth mystery, I reread Nancy's ninth mystery, *The Sign of the Twisted Candles*. I realized that Nancy was still with me.

I write chicklit mysteries. That's a marketing label for women's crime fiction. Whatever you call it, Nancy was the forerunner of chicklit. Consider these elements in *Twisted*:

- *Shopping*. A man may blurt out a clue over a beer, but when a woman tries on a dress, she bares all. Shopping is not frivolous. It's a female bonding ritual. Nancy invites the orphaned Carol into her world with, "Let's go downtown on a shopping spree!"
- *Interrogation technique*. Nancy does her questioning over tea. This cozy approach seems more sensible than the hardboiled method of beating and bullying.
- *Women friends*. Nancy goes everywhere with her female friends, Bess and George. They give her a mystery, then become part of the problem. They may lose an inheritance if Nancy continues her investigation. Nancy doesn't abandon her friends in the name of misplaced honor. Chicklit women know men may leave them, but female friendship is forever.
- *Cars*. Hot cars are a chicklit staple. Nancy drove a roadster first, then later a convertible. Like many chicklit heroines, she has a heavy foot, but she can handle her iron — and change the tires.
- *Attitude*. Nancy is fearless. She orders around the "suave, sleek" crook Jemitt and attacks his abusive wife "with the

speed of a panther." Critics snicker because the police and other important adults listen to Nancy. But it makes sense. Nancy says at least five times, "My father is Carson Drew, the attorney." That's code for "We have money and influence." Chicklit women know their own power.

- *Men.* Both Nancy's father and her boyfriend are support-ive. Chicklit women wouldn't have it any other way. After a night with kidnappers and crooks, Ned says, "One thing that makes you so interesting, Nancy, is that I never know, when I ask you to go out, what mystery will come our way!"

There's more — enough to fill a novel, or in my case, nine novels. And it's not just me. In women's crime fiction, a sarcastic male always asks the heroine, "Who do you think you are, Nancy Drew?"

The answer is yes.

Elaine Viets writes two series. *Murder Unleashed*, the latest book in the best-selling Dead-End Job series, was published in hardcover in May 2006. *Dying in Style* features Josie Marcus, mystery shopper. Elaine has won the Agatha and Anthony Awards. She lives with her husband, Don Crinklaw, in Fort Lauderdale.

Sharon Fiffer on
Murder Must Advertise by Dorothy L. Sayers (1933)

At 21, with three flannel shirts, some torn jeans, and a dress made out of a lace tablecloth hanging in my tiny closet, I was hired as Marshall Field's "high fashion" writer. I got some mileage out of that title. Make up your own joke.

Norma, the experienced writer about fifteen years my senior who sat next to me, was an avid reader. She volunteered to show me the ropes at lunch. If we finished writing our two 10-25 word newspaper gems, we were free to roam the retail fantasy world that was the State Street Marshall Field's. Most days, we ended up at Books on Three. The book department, all pillars and marble floors, maintained the hush and formality of a library without a possessive librarian or a dog-eared copy in sight. Fresh, shiny, colorful books everywhere we looked. Heaven. Norma kept up on the newest releases. Every few weeks she whipped out her employee ID, and, using her discount, purchased hardcover books. I viewed this as a great luxury, especially when I realized that Norma bought mostly mysteries.

"What do you read, then, if you don't read mysteries?" asked Norma when she saw my slightly upturned nose. "Well, literature, I guess," I answered.

Norma froze me out after that remark for a few days, then came in one morning and tossed a book on my desk. "See if this one meets your standards."

Murder Must Advertise by Dorothy L. Sayers. Never heard of it, but I decided I should at least give it a try.

Sayers' detective, Lord Peter Wimsey, was erudite and amusing, a listener, a problem solver — all worthy qualities in a hero. Working undercover at Pym's Publicity as Mr. Death Bredon, Wimsey struggled with advertising slogans, as did I, and murder, which I luckily avoided while working at Marshall Field's.

The eye-opener, however, was Sayers' writing. Smart, clever and soundly plotted, the book satisfied my thirst for classics, "Literature," as I had so naively put it to Norma. *Murder Must Advertise* became my reading link to college years and my reading bridge into the world. Wimsey was the hero who could enter a chaotic world and set it right — something I still crave as a reader and struggle to make happen as a writer.

I left Marshall Field's after two years and lost track of Norma. After a few more years, I went to graduate school, then taught and wrote "literary" short stories and co-edited a fiction magazine, Other Voices, for eight years.

Seven years ago, I began writing a novel about a woman reaching midlife, wondering how she got there and where she was going. Nothing new. The woman worked in advertising. No surprise: write what you know and all that. But to my complete amazement, by the end of the first chapter, my heroine, Jane Wheel, had been fired, kissed her neighbor's husband and found a dead body. I wanted to write about a woman caught in midlife with family and friends, and found the best way to allow her to experience inner growth and discovery was to give her a problem outside herself. Give Jane Wheel a chaotic world to set right.

A few years ago, I ran into an acquaintance from my literary magazines days. She asked me in a supercilious voice if it were true what she heard. "You're writing what ... mysteries now?" I smiled. Her expression had to be just what mine was all those years ago when I turned my nose up at the detective novel in Marshall Field's book department. I nodded. Thanks, Norma.

Sharon Fiffer co-edited three collections of memoirs, *Home, Family* and *Body*, before finding her inner Nancy Drew and writing *Killer Stuff*, the first of her Jane Wheel mysteries. Her fifth book in the series, *Hollywood Stuff*, was published by Minotaur in 2006.

Laura Lippman on
The Postman Always Rings Twice by James M. Cain (1934)

They say you can't judge a book by its cover, but I might not have found James M. Cain without the striking looks that

Vintage used when it reissued six of his titles in the late 1970s. The suggestive, sepia-hued illustrations wrapped around the front and back, hinting at the twists inside. (Turn over *Mildred Pierce*, in fact, and you'll discover a flat-out spoiler.) I started with Cain's first, *The Postman Always Rings Twice*, and spent a semester of college in thrall to his work, despite having little time for discretionary reading.

Flash forward to 1994. I was working — secretly, furtively — on my first novel and trying to improve my lot at The Baltimore Sun, where I felt a bit lost since a merger had thrown the evening paper's scrappy underdogs in with the more sedate morning staffers. Scratching around for stories, I learned that the 60th anniversary of *The Postman Always Rings Twice* was near. Newspapers love anniversaries and *Postman* had a strong local angle to boot: Cain was a Baltimore native and Sun reporter before breaking out as a novelist. I took a flier on the story, reporting it in my spare time, much as I crammed my early reading of Cain into hours I didn't have.

That article changed my life, helping me land a different job at the newspaper. But *Postman* transformed Cain's life far more radically. In fact, as Cain's biographer, Roy Hoopes, told me back then, it's hard to overstate how hard *Postman* hit the public imagination. The book was a bestselling sensation, hailed by most critics, adapted for the stage and screen. Even those rare reviewers who disliked it conceded that *Postman* was an original, visceral work.

Postman has aged well. Although Cain disdained the "hard-boiled" label, it's so tight and lean that it feels like a 500-page manuscript cooked down to the marrow. Cain's lightning-fast prose still has the ability to shock, especially in the whiff of sadomasochism between drifter Frank Chambers and his lover, Cora Papadakis. "[H]er lips stuck out in a way that made me want to mash them in for her," he thinks at first sight of her. The story is a classic noir: Frank gets away with one murder, but is convicted of a killing that was truly an accident. The only off note, to modern ears, is Cain's ugly stereotype of Cora's husband, Nick, a buffoonish Greek immigrant who speaks in pidgin English.

The novel's brilliance lies in the aftermath of Nick Papadakis' murder. The wild, wanton Cora is suddenly all pragmatic domesticity, which unnerves Frank. *Postman* can be read as an allegory about courtship, marriage, and the masculine fear of domestication. (Can it be a coincidence that Frank has a fling with a lion tamer?) The two lovers find it almost impossible to trust one another. After all, once you've killed for someone, it's not much of a leap to kill that person as well.

Cain rang this bell again in *Double Indemnity*, but I prefer *Postman's* more ambiguous take. And I'm glad that Cain dropped his working title. Given that I clearly rely on first impressions, I might not have been as readily drawn to a novel called *Bar-B-Q*.

Laura Lippman's work has won the Edgar, Anthony, Agatha, Shamus and Nero Wolfe awards. She was the first-ever recipient of the Baltimore Mayor's Award for Literary Excellence and the first genre writer chosen as "Author of the Year" by the Maryland Library Association. She lives in Baltimore.

Barbara D'Amato on
Murder on the Orient Express by Agatha Christie (1934)

It would be wonderful to present a scholarly disquisition on revenge fiction — the samurai tale *47 Ronin, Medea, The Count of Monte Cristo*, Poe's "Hopfrog" and more — to its culmination in *Murder on the Orient Express*. But I'm afraid this is an intensely personal account.

I had spent high school and college reading "improving"

books and somewhat bought into the idea that mystery fiction was a lesser cousin. Well, one gets one's comeuppance.

Many years ago I was pregnant and very sick. Nausea all day and night, month after month. I was down to ninety-six pounds. I will spare you the details of — ugh.

One day my husband brought home *Murder on the Orient Express*. He thought it would take my mind off my misery, and it did.

Three hours out of Belgrade, in the middle of the night, the Istanbul-Trieste-Calais train bogs down in a snowbank between Vincovci and Brod. In the morning, a Mr. Ratchett is found dead, stabbed a dozen times. Ratchett, it turns out, is the alias of an infamous kidnapper, guilty of the kidnapping and death of three-year-old Daisy Armstrong. Some of the dozen passengers knew the Armstrongs. Some say they did not. No one can have left the train in the night, as the snow all around is deep and unbroken. Rescue of the train may take hours or days, but as it happens, M. Hercule Poirot is on board.

Who killed Ratchett? His secretary? Or Russian Princess Dragomiroff? Meek Swedish nurse Greta Ohlsson? The English governess Mary Debenham? Or one of the others?

The moment I began reading, I knew I was in the hands of a master. Since I came to Agatha Christie with no knowledge of her books or her program of violating *fairly* all the rules of the Detection Club and S.S. Van Dine's even stricter list, I had no idea what the ending would be.

But the reading of it was wonderful. Such clean, straightforward prose. Unblinking and direct. No fancy flourishes, no lavishing attention on the scenery for its own sake. No filler, no padding. The story was developed almost entirely through conversation, and therefore I had to believe I was getting the straight facts — always allowing for the obvious fact that at least one of the characters must be lying — and yet I was being very cleverly deceived. As Poirot said, "Sometimes I am haunted by the sensation that really it must be very simple." And it was.

Plus, Christie has a subtle, wry sense of humor. Rereading *Murder on the Orient Express* recently, I was amused to find the sleeping car attendant, who had a very painful toothache, say "I turned on my light and continued to read — to take my mind off, as it were."

While I was reading *Orient Express* I was unaware of how sick I felt. Of course, being crisply and efficiently written, it ended all too soon. Never a slow thinker, my husband brought home another Christie, and then several more. I wish there had been several hundred.

Now I reread the Marples and the Poirots every ten years or so. It's amazing how well they hold up. They're so organic that I know who did it, of course, but it's fun to watch the master at work. It was many years before I got up the nerve to try writing a mystery myself, but the love for the genre had been firmly established.

By the way, the baby who started my interest, now fully adult, published a novel a few years ago and is working on his second.

I suppose there's no connection.

Barbara D'Amato has won the Carl Sandburg Award for Fiction, the Macavity, Agatha, Anthony, Readers' Choice Awards and others. She is a past president of Mystery Writers of America and Sisters in Crime International. A native of Michigan, she has lived for many years in Chicago. Her most recent novel is *Death of a Thousand Cuts*.

Edward Hoch on
The Chinese Orange Mystery by Ellery Queen (1934)

When I was nine years old, the furthest thing from my mind was becoming a professional writer, to say nothing of a mystery writer! But on Sunday nights I often listened, along with my parents, to *The Adventures of Ellery Queen* on CBS Radio. These mysteries, with their fair-play clues and Challenge to the Listener, both interested and intrigued me. Later in that fateful year of 1939, when most adult eyes were turned toward Europe, I happened to walk into a Walgreen drug store in downtown Rochester, New York, and see a display of Pocket Books with their eye-catching laminated covers. They were the first paper-backs to be published in America and I had to own one. Clutching my quarter, I considered James Hilton and Agatha Christie before settling on the name I knew best — Ellery Queen.

That book, *The Chinese Orange Mystery*, was the first adult book I ever read. I will not pretend it to be Ellery Queen's best novel. In fact, I would not even rank it among his ten best. But at that moment in my life its bizarre crime and intricate solution fueled the fire of my imagination. It concerned an unknown man found murdered in an office waiting room, his clothes on backwards, his tie missing, and two African spears stuck up his pant legs and shirt like ramrods. Why had the killer taken the time and trouble to set the scene like this, who was the man, and why did nobody know him? I suspected the book's title may hold the key to it, but what was the meaning of the Chinese Orange?

I tried to puzzle this out along with Ellery, but failed miserably. I knew from the radio show that the least likely suspect was often the killer, but in this case I couldn't decide on a least likely suspect. Late in the book, when the dead man's suitcase is discovered, I read through the entire list of its contents and missed the extremely clever negative clue that pointed toward the dead man's identity. Needless to say, I was a failure as a detective — but not as a reader. Over the next few years I sought out every Ellery Queen novel as it appeared in paperback, then went on to Conan Doyle and many others. By the time I was fifteen, I'd joined a mystery book club and become a regular reader of Ellery Queen's Mystery Magazine. At age seventeen, while still in high school, I decided to become a writer. It was no surprise when, after years of trying, my mysteries were the stories that sold first.

Today I would advise readers to begin the Ellery Queen saga with *Cat of Many Tails* or *Calamity Town*. But for me, back when I was nine years old, there was only one book — *The Chinese Orange Mystery*.

Edward D. Hoch is past president of Mystery Writers of America and recipient of its Edgar and Grand Master Awards. Twice winner of the Anthony Award, he has also received Bouchercon's Lifetime Achievement Award. Author of over 900 published short stories, he has appeared in every issue of Ellery Queen's Mystery Magazine for the past 33 years. His latest collection is *More Things Impossible* (Crippen & Landru).

Sally Wright on
The Nine Tailors by Dorothy L. Sayers (1934)

I was a weird kid. I liked Shakespeare and Suetonius, because they were read to me. I never understood what a cootie was. Kids thought I was peculiar.

I took up residence in fantasyland with Dickens, with Merlin, with *Rebecca*'s replacement, with *The Man In The Iron Mask*, pecking out tacky stories. Then I got to high school, and Dorothy L. Sayers made me want to write mysteries.

She created a character who grew into a person in her own lushly detailed world in 1920s England. She told crafted tales with innovative style in a feisty, descriptive, amused voice. For, unlike those of her contemporaries, most of Sayers' mysteries are real novels of character and manners that live and breathe on their own.

Lord Peter Wimsey is the soul inside the stories — his gentlemanly self-mockery, his regard for all sorts, his breadth of knowledge and ability, and his single-minded search for truth no matter who it hurts. He's a man of parts who detests pretension, an aristocrat of substance inside a whimsical slip-cover. Sayers' concerns are moral: guilt, justice, personal responsibility, the value of work well done.

Wimsey lives in an age of war-wounded without work, of Bolshevik clubs and vapid flappers, of women fighting for jobs and education — all caught in the never-ending struggle between what's good and what's evil. Sayers reveals that social setting with compassion *and* acerbic wit, sprinkled with scholarly snobbery. Peter actually proposes (and Harriet Vane accepts) in untranslated Latin — after three books chronicling their courtship! Which still rankles today.

But I do like the learning in Sayers' books, like the campanology in *The Nine Tailors* — the bells, the ringers, the terminology, all of which Sayers studied exhaustively. She already knew the social context (the clerical circle of a small village parish in the flat, dike-crossed Fens), since her father had been rector of just such a village. Sayers makes the country, the people and the action real in a degree remarkable for her time — the rector and his wife in particular. Though when Wimsey applies the pattern of a "peal" to decrypt a critical clue, Sayers, being a woman of excess (gastronomical *and* literary), presents *every* detail.

Even so, she opened a door for the rest of us by describing work in depth, and plenty have walked through (Dick Francis among them). It was that, and her "novel of manners as mystery" that changed the genre forever — and helped make me a novelist writing the Ben Reese books.

Like Wimsey, Ben knows what war's like. He was a scout in WWII who became a college archivist restoring books and paintings. He was born poor on a Michigan farm, but he suffers from a form of limitless curiosity that's not unlike Wimsey's. Their personalities are totally different, but they both hate cruelty *and* hypocrisy. And expect a lot of themselves.

Reese gives me challenges and satisfactions much as Wimsey must've given Sayers: immersion in an interesting male mind in depth from book to book; a reason to learn new undertakings while shaking my head at human nature; a chance to examine death and sorrow, as well as justice and mercy.

C.S. Lewis said Dorothy L. Sayers "... aspired to be, and was, at once a popular entertainer and a conscientious craftsman: like (in her degree) Chaucer, Cervantes, Shakespeare, or Moliere. I have an idea that, with a very few exceptions, it is only such writers who matter much in the long run."

Even her detractors say Sayers was brilliant, with her plays, her Christian apologetics and her translation of Dante.

But I, for one, still find myself wishing she'd written more Peter Wimseys.

Sally Wright, a 2001 Edgar finalist, has studied rare books, early explorers, painting restoration, exotic toxins, army life in World War II, plus Scotland, England, Malaya and Italy to write her books about Ben Reese, a university archivist and former-World War II Scout.

Gillian Roberts on
Fer-de-Lance by Rex Stout (1934)

I was seduced by Archie Goodwin.

Before him, I was a mystery virgin. My parents' house was filled with books, but none were mysteries, and Nancy Drew was persona non grata on the shelves of the Philadelphia library system. (She wasn't welcomed there until the '90s, as I recall.) My reading lists in high school and college were devoid of anything resembling a mystery except for a few short stories by Poe.

Not until years later, when I was heady with freedom as somebody else entertained my toddlers during story hour, did I venture into the exotic territory of the mystery section of the library. Revelation!

This was in the dark ages before American women's mysteries had burst on the scene, humanizing and enlarging the scope of the genre. Back then, the mystery world I'd "discovered" seemed divided between class-conscious British puzzlers with vicars and country homes and American tales of tough loners roaming still-tougher streets. I read about those detectives; I didn't identify with them.

And then I read *Fer-de-Lance* by Rex Stout and was captivated. His puzzles were as clever as Christie's, and Archie was tough and toted a gun when necessary. But physical violence wasn't always required, the criminals weren't primarily gangsters and thugs, and there was always an element of hope. These books have an undercurrent of joy in life and while Archie might be cynical, his outlook isn't bleak and disillusioned.

Most of all, these detectives were accessible. As eccentric as Nero Wolfe was, he had a life — a history, a house, a past — and an ongoing idiosyncratic set of obsessions — orchids and gourmet fare — that had nothing to do with criminal pursuits. In fact, the criminals were pursued in order to pay for the interests.

They weren't isolates, either. It's an odd family under that roof on West 35th Street, but what else would you call Nero and Archie and their housemates, the cook Fritz, the orchid keeper Horstmann plus the visiting relatives — that recurring crew of outside detectives? From the first in the series, *Fer-de-Lance*, it's made clear that Nero and Archie have a long-standing relationship of mutual respect and trust — at least when they are not annoying or infuriating each other. They're much like the members of any other family.

And then, of course, there's Archie himself, the wise-cracking, self-deprecating, insightful narrator of the stories. He's there for the reader in a way few other detectives of the time seemed to be. He's smart, but not superhuman, and he shares his confusion, disappointment, boredom, annoyance and enthusiasm with the reader, and gives his emotions a twist of good-natured humor. He's Everyman.

Archie inspires affection and admiration, not awe, so it's easy to identify with him and to be fully engaged in the story. It worked for me back then, and after recently rereading *Fer-de-Lance*, it still does.

To me, Stout combined and realigned the mannered English puzzle and the American duke-it-out adventures of a cowboy-knight and with this trans-Atlantic feat, he opened the genre to wide possibilities.

I fell in love with Archie Goodwin, with the idea of "voice" and with the mystery itself as soon as I opened *Fer-de-Lance*. There seemed no point in resisting. There still doesn't.

Beginning with Anthony winner, *Caught Dead in Philadelphia*, **Gillian Roberts'** high school English teacher, Amanda Pepper, and homicide-cop turned grad student, C. K. Mackenzie, have been at the center of thirteen City of Brotherly Love crimes, most recently, *Till the End of Tom* and *A Hole in Juan*.

Dick Lochte on
The Saint in New York by Leslie Charteris (1935)

More than 40 years ago, I discovered a hardcover copy of the
first book-length American adventure of Leslie Charteris'
popular modern Robin Hood, Simon Templar. It had rested,
undisturbed and out of print, for some time beneath a stack of
old Life magazines in the back of a junk shop in the French
Quarter of New Orleans (an establishment that I suppose is
gone now, like much of my beloved hometown). It was marked
25¢ but it would have been inexpensive at any price.

It was, and is, an ideal choice for an introduction to the Saint
series, thanks to a prologue in the form of a letter sent from
Chief Inspector Claude Eustace Teal of Scotland Yard to New
York's Police Commissioner warning him of Templar's presence
in Manhattan. It provides the commissioner and the reader with
a detailed description of the hero ("Age 31. Height 6 ft. 2 ins.
Weight 173 lbs. Eyes blue. Hair black.") and his special
characteristics ("Always immaculately dressed. Luxurious
tastes. Known as 'The Saint' from habit of leaving drawing of
skeleton figure with halo on scenes of crimes.").

Included also is Templar's "Record," which smartly sums
up the earlier novels in the series. And, to slide the reader neatly
into this one, there's mention of a warning The Saint has sent
to Irboll, a thug on trial for killing a cop. If Irboll is acquitted,
which seems likely considering the judge is bought and the jury
stacked, Templar vows to administer his own brand of justice.

From there, Charteris takes us into the book proper, with a
droll description of a nun entering the tower suite of the Waldorf
Astoria, catching a toe in a rug and saying, "'God damn!' in a
distinctly male baritone ..." It is, of course, The Saint, fresh from
shooting Irboll. "I caught him as he came out [of the court-
house]," he tells the man responsible for his stateside journey.
"Just once. Then I let out a thrilling scream and rushed towards

him. I was urging him to repent and confess his sins while they were looking for me. There was quite a crowd around, and I think nearly all of them were arrested."

What adventure-hungry teenager (or gray-haired adult) wouldn't find such outrageous behavior completely irresistible? The novel becomes even more appealing as Charteris unveils what is arguably his cleanest and shrewdest plot. The Saint is in New York at the behest of wealthy industrialist William Valcross who, seeking vengeance for the kidnapping and murder of his son, has convinced the Brighter Buccaneer to rid the city of its most prominent criminals.

With wit, élan and no small degree of violence, the Saint, beating Richard Stark's (Donald Westlake's) antihero Parker to the punch by nearly three decades, works his way up through the organized crime hierarchy until, finally, he faces Mr. Big.

By contemporary standards, the novel may strike some as being the result of a young writer too fond of his creation. The Saint is a bit too perfect when compared to the drunks and losers and whiners that constitute today's fictional crimefighting elite. Charteris was in his twenties when he wrote the book and was clearly under the sway of such Brit adventure titans as Edgar Wallace, E.W. Hornung (Raffles) and H.C. McNeile (Bulldog Drummond). But he was a more effective writer than they, with a vocabulary second only to S.J. Perelman's and, like Perelman, was blessed with a humorist's heart.

The Saint in New York showed me how a crime novel could be hardboiled and humorous, adventurous and mysterious, filled with action, and yet pack a who-done-it surprise punch. But, most of all, it still serves as a prime example of how much pure fun a mystery can and should be.

Dick Lochte's novels have been nominated for nearly every mystery book award and have been translated into more than a dozen languages. His *Sleeping Dog* won the Nero Wolfe Award and was selected one of the 100 Favorite Mysteries of the Century by the Independent Mystery Booksellers Association. His latest novel is *Croaked!* (Five Star, 2006).

Parnell Hall on
The Case of the Counterfeit Eye by Erle Stanley Gardner (1935)

I grew up on Erle Stanley Gardner. My parents were English lit teachers, and after a hard day of slogging through the classics, they would come home, put their feet up, and whip out a copy of the latest Perry Mason novel. As a young lad I was intrigued by this strange phenomenon, so one day I picked up a copy of *The Case of the Counterfeit Eye*.

That book knocked my socks off. Never mind the courtroom drama — which was absolutely great, by the way. What blew me away was the character of Mason himself. Because in the early books — and *Counterfeit Eye* is one of the earliest — before there was a TV show, Mason was always doing such outrageous, outlandish and downright illegal things, that the mystery was not whodunit, so much as how-will-he-get-away-with-it.

In *The Case of the Counterfeit Eye* (Gardner's titles grab you before you even open the book), Mason's client is a one-eyed man whose specially made bloodshot glass eye has been stolen, and an inferior (counterfeit) eye left in its place. Naturally, the real eye turns up on the body of a murdered man and Mason's client is thrown in jail.

How does Perry Mason protect his client? Just the way any lawyer would. He has a half a dozen bloodshot glass eyes made, and plants one on the next body he finds!

Next, he hires a starving actress, sends her to Reno, and has her served divorce papers in the name of a key witness who skipped out. When the district attorney has the woman extradited, and accuses Mason of spiriting her out of the jurisdiction of the court, Mason advises her not to talk. The prosecutor is livid, and the judge is moved to remark, "Counselor, the Court is beginning to believe that you are instructing this witness not to answer questions... not because you feel the answers may incriminate *her*, but because you feel that the answers may incriminate *you*."

This was, of course, an elaborate stunt. But Mason would think nothing of actually tampering with a witness. Or firing a few extra bullets around at a crime scene to make the ballistic expert jump through hoops. Or snatching a piece of evidence before the police could find it.

As a ten-year-old boy, I found this mind blowing. I was hooked and hooked good.

The Counterfeit Eye was just the tip of the iceberg. There are 82 Perry Mason books, and I have read every one of them several times.

When Erle Stanley Gardner died in 1970, I applied to Gardner's widow for permission to write a Perry Mason novel. She replied, "You creepy kid, what makes you think you could do that?" though in much kinder terms. Unfortunately, by the time her letter reached me I was already 150 pages into *The Case of the Anonymous Client*. I was crushed, but I set the manuscript aside and never completed it.

In 1987, my first book, *Detective*, was published. It was a private eye novel, but that didn't matter. Once you're published, you can get published. I dusted off my old manuscript. I still couldn't write a Perry Mason novel, but maybe I could adapt it. Unfortunately, the premise of the book required that the lawyer be an established character. But I had a screenplay, *The Baxter Trust*, about a young hippie lawyer that I had written as a star vehicle for myself back in my old acting days. I adapted it as a novel, got a two book deal, and the second book in the

69

series, *The Anonymous Client*, a Steve Winslow courtroom drama, was the old Perry Mason novel I'd begun over 15 years before.

I would never have written *The Anonymous Client* if I had not read *The Case of the Counterfeit Eye.*

I probably never would have written *Detective* either.

Parnell Hall is the author of five Steve Winslow courtroom dramas written under the pseudonym J.P. Hailey. Under his own name, he is the author of the Stanley Hastings private eye novels and the Puzzle Lady crossword puzzle mysteries. *You Have the Right to Remain Puzzled* is due in Fall 2006.

Jeanne M. Dams on
Gaudy Night by Dorothy L. Sayers (1935)

I remember distinctly the first time I read a Sayers novel. I was 26-years-old and was, for some reason, a counselor at a summer camp run by the Episcopal Church. (It's hard to imagine a less likely camp counselor than I, but that's beside the point.) I went into the office one day and found the priest in charge of the camp sitting all by himself roaring with laughter over a book he was reading. It was a paperback of Sayers' *Clouds of Witness.* The priest lent me the book later — and changed my life.

I got all the Sayers books I could find at the library and devoured them. They were just then, in the late '60s, being reissued, so I haunted bookstores in both America and the UK until I owned all the mysteries. I read them and reread them until I could quote whole paragraphs. (Still can. Don't get me started.) I made one of my sisters read them, too, and I'll never forget the evening she called me, just having finished *Gaudy Night.* "Okay, dammit," she said without preliminaries, "did he propose again and did she accept? It's in Latin, for God's sake!"

As Peter and Harriet went on, after the exchange of Latin, to embarrass an Oxford proctor by "closely and passionately embracing...right under the Warden's windows," I told Ruth I assumed they had reached an agreement. I didn't know it at the time, but I had reached an epiphany.

I reread *Gaudy Night* once, twice, a dozen times. I gloried in the Oxford atmosphere, the civilized discourse. I talked, over the years, with other Sayers fans and learned of the Dorothy L. Sayers Society, which I immediately joined. From them I learned of her theological works, learned that she was one of the great lay Christian apologists of her day, right up there with C.S. Lewis (with whom she carried on an extensive correspondence). I read, again and again in various books and plays and pamphlets, her insistence on the moral obligation of doing one's "proper job," a precept I had first seen articulated in *Gaudy Night*.

I knew I wasn't doing my proper job. I had been trained as an elementary school teacher, a profession at which I was abysmally bad. I went from there to various jobs, none of them very satisfactory. Working in a killer job as a university administrator, I kept rereading Sayers and especially *Gaudy Night*. How I loved those oh-so-English mysteries!

I'm not always very quick on the uptake. It took me way too long to figure out that since I loved Sayers, knew the English mystery inside out, and could write competent English, maybe it would make sense to try to write some English detective fiction.

I didn't know if I could write fiction, but I was determined to try. Eventually I finished my first book, got it published, won an award and I was off.

Fourteen books later, I think I am finally doing my proper job. Oh, it doesn't pay me enough to live on. These days I have to do a lot of other things to make ends meet, but I know beyond doubt that writing is my vocation. It pleases me.

Oh, by the way, those Latin lines in *Gaudy Night*? They are the question and response given at Oxford degree-granting ceremonies. "Placetne, magister?" the Chancellor of the University is asked. Does it please you (to award degrees to these candidates)? And he replies "Placet." It pleases me.

A certain symmetry, isn't there?

Jeanne M. Dams has written nine books starring Dorothy Martin, American widow living and sleuthing in England, and five about Hilda Johansson, Swedish housemaid to the powerful Studebaker family of South Bend, Indiana, in the early twentieth century. The most recent titles are *Winter of Discontent* (Dorothy) and *Crimson Snow* (Hilda).

Valerie S. Malmont on
The Burning Court by John Dickson Carr (1937)

Memory can play funny tricks on people. What one remembers is not necessarily fact.

When I was eleven years old, I lived on a remote island in the Pacific, where I had recently worked my way through our small Navy library's entire collection of British Golden Age mystery writers. I'd gone from Allingham to Upfield and felt there was nothing left.

Then my mother suggested I read *The Burning Court*. It immediately became my favorite book of all time. It is one of two books I wish I had been able to write. (The other is *The Haunting of Hill House* by Shirley Jackson, which should be the subject of another essay.)

When I was asked to write about a mystery that had influenced me, the first book that came to mind was *The Burning Court*. I recalled that I loved it because it was a beautifully written, classic locked room mystery, with supernatural elements skillfully blended in, and with a baffling and ambiguous ending. To prepare myself, I reread the book in the same paperback edition I'd read as a child: a 1944 Popular Library edition, the original cost of which was 25¢!

My first surprise was the print was a lot smaller than I remembered.

A much bigger surprise was the setting. In my younger days, I assumed the setting was an English village with some of the backstory taking place years earlier in France. Carr's descriptions of an ancient mansion, a country cottage and a small village, and even his use of language, seemed to be typically British.

Now I live in Pennsylvania, and I was startled to discover the story took place, not in an English village, but instead in an American village between Ardmore and Bryn Mawr along the Philadelphia Main Line. There is even a reference in the book to the famous Pennsylvania Dutch Hex murder, which took place in 1928, only a year before the events in the novel occurred.

I should not have been so surprised for Carr was born in Pennsylvania. However, Carr lived in England for many years and absorbed the culture and rhythms of the English language as spoken in Great Britain.

One place my memory did not fail me was about the French background of the novel. The backstory did take place in France, where the protagonist Edward Stevens met his wife, the mysterious and beautiful Marie D'Aubray.

As the book opens, Stevens, an editor at a large publishing house, is given a manuscript about famous poisoners by noted historian Gaudan Cross. Glancing over the manuscript while on a train heading toward his weekend home, he is shocked to find in it a photograph of a famous poisoner who was guillotined in France in 1861. She looks exactly like Edward's wife, and is shown wearing a bracelet identical to one his wife often wears. But the most amazing coincidence is the poisoner's name: Marie D'Aubray.

An old friend, Dr. Welden, who is also on the train and whose hobby is studying noted murders, recalls another poisoner with the name Marie D'Aubray, better known as the Marquise de Brinvilliers. For her crimes of poisoning relatives and acquaintances with arsenic, she was tortured and burnt in 1676.

The action starts immediately, with not one but two impossible locked room situations: an arsenic poisoning in a bedroom and the disappearance of a body from a crypt. The detective is the improbable Gaudan Cross, who manages to explain everything so well that the reader says, "Of course — why didn't I see that?" But there is an unexpected twist during the grand denouement and a stranger twist in the stunning epilogue that will leave the reader wondering forever what really happened.

And it is that sense of wonder that stayed with me all these years and made *The Burning Court* one of the most influential books I have ever read. More than half a century after it was written it is still a fascinating and unforgettable story.

Valerie S. Malmont is the author of five mystery novels and one novella featuring Tori Miracle, a foreign Service brat, who is transplanted to rural Pennsylvania and suffers culture shock. Valerie has lived on the islands of Okinawa and Taiwan, and in Laos. She has a degree in Archaeology and a Masters of Librarianship.

Roberta Gellis on
Busman's Honeymoon by Dorothy L. Sayers (1937)

When I was asked about which of the classic mysteries had influenced my work, my first reaction was a sort of indignant rejection — as if I were suspected of lacking originality and needed to lean on the past. My second was rather shamefaced laughter at such utter vanity. I had been an avid reader since about five years of age; how could it be possible that ingesting (and I use the word advisedly because as a young reader I did seem to swallow books whole) would not have molded my pattern of thinking as I absorbed them?

I read everything and anything, but I always enjoyed the mystery genre and always read it. Nonetheless, when I came to think seriously about the influence of mysteries I had read in the past and reread recently, because it is my habit to reread favorite works, I simply could not pick an outstanding work. Other factors were determining: (1) that I knew nothing about modern forensics and (2) the operation of modern law enforcement and the judicial system were closed books to me. More important, since research could solve both those problems, I did not want to learn about them.

That set my work firmly in the past and eliminated from my choice of detectives "kick-ass" women. Yet for work set in the past, gender often determines what is possible for a detective to learn. I needed a male/female partnership. I think it was at that point in my planning that the mysteries written by Dorothy Sayers came to my mind. Peter and Harriet, particularly as displayed in *Busman's Honeymoon*, had the kind of relationship that appealed to me and sparked notions of how my hero and heroine could interact.

In *Busman's Honeymoon*, Peter and Harriet are newlyweds. Although they have known each other for years, being bound by law and custom is an entirely new situation for them. Each is acutely aware that the other has sensitivities that must be respected. For example, Harriet was tried for the murder of her lover, and it was Peter who discovered the real murderer and saved her life. Nonetheless she *had* a lover and Peter is anxious about reminding her of that painful episode. Harriet is aware that she has married out of her class and is concerned about not embarrassing Peter.

These anxieties add depth to the characters, being woven by a word, a phrase, through the everyday lives and then the extraordinary experience of discovering a body in the basement of their house. The discovery induces guilt in Harriet because it was she who wanted this house; she keeps wondering whether she should have agreed to a more conventional honeymoon in luxury hotels on the Continent. Peter, wishing to reassure her, is driven to solve the murder, although he assures her that his infernal curiosity would have forced him to investigate anyway.

In 1936 when *Busman's Honeymoon* was probably written (it was published in 1937) the actions allowed different genders were still very distinct. It is, then, Harriet who questions and listens to the women in the story while Peter obtains information from the men. How they combine their information and the uneasiness each feels at disclosing what he or she has learned make Peter and Harriet more human, and showed me how such a situation could be used in my own books.

I believe that the relationship of Peter and Harriet in Dorothy Sayers' work did influence the way I developed the protagonists of the Magdalene la Bâtarde series of mysteries. There could be no question of marriage between Magdalene, who is a whoremistress, and Bell, the bishop's knight, but the fact that they are strongly attracted to each other and *must* work together to solve the crime establishes a relationship a little bit like marriage. Their growing concern for each other is, I think, an essential factor in their success as characters.

Roberta Gellis has been a successful writer of fiction for several decades, having published about 40 novels since 1964. In 2004 Gellis won the Romantic Times award for Best Historical Mystery for *Bone of Contention*, the third book in the Magdalene la Bâtard mystery series. Book four in the series is *Chains of Folly* (Five Star, 2006).

Linda Fairstein on
Rebecca by Daphne du Maurier (1938)

I was thirteen years old when Daphne du Maurier's 1938 classic *Rebecca* was placed in my hands by a librarian. The woman knew my taste in literature and my great affection for mysteries, and she urged me to take the book home for the weekend. I did so reluctantly — the dust jacket had the look of "romantic suspense," which I have never enjoyed — but my trusty guide's comment that it was a perfect Gothic thriller overcame my resistance.

"Last night I dreamt I went to Manderley again" is the famous opening line of this timeless classic. I was drawn in immediately by the intimacy of the first-person point of view as the timid, self-doubting narrator begins her tale with a vision of her return to the stately home where she first came as the young bride of the elegant Maxim de Winter.

The whirlwind Riviera courtship of the couple twists into a dark psychological drama of fear and suspicion back at Manderley — and as unlikely as it seemed in the opening chapters — a tale of murder, too. The protagonist is overwhelmed to find that she is battling the ever-present spirit of the beloved Rebecca — de Winter's late wife — with everyone from her husband to the servants who direct all aspects of her life and to the new friends who surround her. Her constant eagerness to please the difficult Maxim ratchets up to a level of anxiety that is palpable to the reader as du Maurier immerses her terrified narrator in the dark atmosphere of her dazzling predecessor's life.

There were several things about the writing that I have never forgotten. It is this second Mrs. De Winter through whose eyes the story unfolds. We are with her every step of the way, from her first meeting of Maxim through the insidious destruction of her naivete by all those loyal to Rebecca's ghost. I cannot recall another novel in which we are so very close to the storyteller, yet never learn her name. It is, I think, a subtle and enormously effective technique that du Maurier used to underscore the narrator's profound inferiority.

The novel is also remarkable for the strong sense of place at Manderley. This is a book with remarkably little action. But the suspense and the relentlessly increasing atmosphere of doom build steadily from the time that Maxim and his bride first arrive at the great house. Every detail of the Cornwall estate is described, every belonging of the late Rebecca laid out as though to torment the new Mrs. de Winter, creating a richly dense backdrop for the twists that steadily unfold thereafter.

A third thing that du Maurier did so brilliantly was showing the reader, not just telling us, how the narrator's inevitable path to disaster developed. We are with her when she mistakenly enters Rebecca's room for the first time, touching the silk dressing gown, fingering the dead woman's monogram — R de W — woven on the lingerie case, envying the wardrobe full of gold brocade and shimmery silver evening clothes. She is caught in that moment by the sinister Mrs. Danvers, Rebecca's personal maid, who takes her back over each item, forcing her to listen as she describes how beautiful Rebecca looked in the dressing gown and how the "skull-faced" Danvers used to brush her long hair for her every night. Like our story-teller, we feel "deadly sick" about the days to come.

I have gone back to reread *Rebecca* dozens of times over the years, and it has held up with each visit. So I have long considered du Maurier to be one of my personal mystery muses, from the time I first discovered this haunting tale of psychological suspense.

Linda Fairstein served as chief prosecutor of Manhattan's pioneering Sex Crimes Unit for 30 years. She is the *New York Times* bestselling author of the Alexandra Cooper series of crime novels. The eighth book in that series – *Death Dance* — was published by Scribner in 2006.

Nicholas Kilmer
Lament for a Maker by Michael Innes (1938)

When I first laid eyes on El Greco's "View of Toledo" in the Metropolitan Museum of Art in New York (I was about twelve years old), I enjoyed the sensation of being lifted up by the back of the neck, shaken and subjected to a chill of impacted presence so strong that I still cannot account for it. I was floored, flummoxed, amazed and, I suppose, challenged. The painting still thrills me.

Years later a client asked me to buy for him, at auction, a soupy and indistinct landscape into which he was reading considerable possibilities. I warned him away from the purchase with what I hoped was a rhetorical question: "Is it pregnant or are you?" Because a part of what we sense, responding to any stimulus, is based on what we ourselves bring to the experience.

I came upon Michael Innes' *Lament for a Maker* more than 40 years ago when I was in graduate school, studying (I believe that is the word I used for what I was doing) English Literature. While I read it, I experienced again some of the sensations that had so alerted me when confronted with the "View of Toledo."

Innes (under his given name, J.I.M. Stewart), was himself a scholar of English Literature, Oxford don, author of the final volume of *The Oxford Encyclopedia of English Literature*. His book, the first I'd encountered by him, was eloquent of a grand and cranky Scottish landscape rendered almost uninhabitable by snow and ice, with odd and disquieting interruptions of the Australian bush. It was inhabited by memorable stock characters in the persons of Ranald Guthrie, mad laird of Erchany; his evil henchperson Hardcastle; the idiot Daftie Tammas; the sutor Ewan Bell.[1] The ruined castle tottered and stood out against sweeping gestures of weather almost worthy of Tolkien, whom I encountered first at the same time. And, running through the pages as they did through crevices in the ruined castle, were rats, including even "Learned rats. Rats, that is to say, lugging laboriously round with them little paper scrolls — rather like students who have just been given a neatly-printed degree."

This student was beguiled by the musical accuracy of frequent fragments of Scottish dialect, the high degree of literacy exhibited by the author in his narrative, but most especially by the recurring chimes of the Scots poet William Dunbar (1465-1520?), whose dirge runs through the book, giving it not only its color but, finally, its insistent theme, from the poem's final stanza:

> Sen for the deid remeid is none,
>   Best is that we for dede dispone,
> Eftir our deid that lif may we;
>   Timor mortis conturbat me.[2]

---

[1] Read the book patiently and you will learn what a *sutor* is, along with much more dialect, because Innes is a canny teacher.

[2] Online text copyright ©2003 Ian Lancashire for the Department of English, University of Toronto. Dunbar's poem, written while he believed himself to be mortally ill, was first published in 1508. It is a lament for his fellow English and Scots poets who have died. The final stanza may be translated: Since death permits no remedy, / Provide against mortality / That we may live after we die;/ Terror of death bewilders me.

Indeed, I was so taken by Dunbar's poem that, when I remembered what I was supposed to be doing, and cast about for a subject that might lead to a thesis for the doctoral degree, I contemplated working with this poet.[3]

Rereading the book, I was once again lifted and shaken by Dunbar's words, and it was with considerable pleasure that I put aside more pressing tasks in order to wander, with Michael Innes, through his tale. But it was not the book I recalled, except for the weather, the landscape, the dialect, and that magnificent poem. Never mind the story — had those elements alone been enough to justify my first response? — I found myself wondering whether, on that initial reading, the book had been pregnant, or if it was I. If the latter, I want to acknowledge the book's role as midwife, because Innes' *Lament for a Maker* provides an example I mean to follow, in which beauty and erudition rest comfortably within the matrix of a modest fiction.

Nicholas Kilmer's *Madonna of the Apes* was published by Poisoned Pen Press in 2005. It is the sixth in a series of art mysteries. Kilmer makes his living as an art dealer. Poems of his have recently been published by The Paris Review, Salma-gundi, Western Humanities Review and Arion.

Jon L. Breen on
Dance of Death by Helen McCloy (1938)

Why is the body of a young woman, found buried in a Fifth Avenue snowdrift, hot to the touch? This seeming impossibility opens one of the finest first novels of its time and a landmark of formal detective fiction.

---

[3] Ultimately those who tie such degrees around the necks of deserving rats failed to so burden mine.

If the Golden Age of Detection is defined as the period between the two World Wars, Helen McCloy barely makes the cut. But *Dance of Death* placed her in the honorable company of such American classics as S.S. Van Dine, Ellery Queen, John Dickson Carr, Anthony Abbot, Anthony Boucher, Clyde B. Clason, Stuart Palmer, Clayton Rawson and C. Daly King.

The influence of McCloy's contemporaries is clear from the start. An opening disclaimer promises fair play: "No scientific knowledge is needed for the solution of the crime, beyond that which is given in the course of the narrative, before the solution is reached." A list of the significant clues precedes the solution. The characters and setting are mostly upper crust, centered around a debutante dance. There are enough art and literary references for a Philo Vance or Lord Peter Wimsey novel. As in Queen and Van Dine, the detective's association with the highest levels of law enforcement (in Dr. Basil Willing's case as a psychiatric consultant to the District Attorney's office) gives him entrée to the investigation. As in Van Dine and Abbot, the Police Commissioner and District Attorney wander around on the front lines of the investigation.

Willing, aged between 40 and 50, got his medical training at Johns Hopkins after World War I. He is multilingual and half Russian on his mother's side. He lives in "an antiquated house at the unfashionable end of Park Avenue, below Grand Central," where we meet him in after-dinner conversation, trying to convince the Commissioner that all police should read Freud. Willing goes on to assert his sleuthing credo: "Every criminal leaves psychic fingerprints." Many earlier fictional detectives had talked a lot about psychology (Philo Vance for one) or based their solutions on Freudian themes (Edwin Balmer and William MacHarg's Luther Trant, Arthur B. Reeve's Craig Kennedy), but as one of the first psychiatrist sleuths, Willing turned the psychology up a notch in depth and sophistication, serving as a transitional figure from Golden Age puzzles to

1940s psychological suspense.

The Freudian reasoning that leads Willing to his solution might be considered simplistic, or even discredited, by a present-day practitioner. But it represents the thinking of the time and is beautifully integrated into the puzzle plot, its concepts explained well in advance in fairness to the reader.

Though McCloy was belatedly awarded the Grand Master by the Mystery Writers of America in 1990, her later work, always professional but inferior to her best work of the '30s and '40s, may have tarnished her reputation. Changing fashions caused her to stop writing about Willing in the 1950s, returning to him only occasionally while producing books that were more pure suspense than classical detection.

One reason I am so enthusiastic about McCloy is a revelation that came to me some time in the late 1960s during my Army service. In a downcast mood, I sat in a library (it may have been a public library in Washington, DC, or a post library in San Antonio or in Vietnam — I'm not sure) and read a novel by Helen McCloy. When I'd finished, I realized that a well-wrought example of the Golden Age puzzle-spinner's art had the power to cheer me up. I'm not sure *Dance of Death* was the novel, but it easily might have been.

Jon L. Breen, author of six novels and 90-plus short stories, has won two Edgar Awards in the biographical/critical category. His lastest book is *Kill the Umpire: The Calls of Ed Gorgon* (Crippen & Landru) and his novel, *Eye of God*, is coming in 2006 from Perseverance Press.

Lyn Hamilton on
The Mask of Dimitrios aka A Coffin for Dimitrios by Eric Ambler (1939)

For someone raised, as I was, to believe mysteries are solved in English villages, manor houses, or brownstones in New York, Eric Ambler's *The Mask of Dimitrios* came as a revelation. The fictional world to which I had been exposed up until then (I was thirteen or fourteen at the time) was essentially a moral or at least a benign one, the murderer an aberration to be revealed both cleverly and expeditiously so that the universe could continue to unfold as it should.

The elements I had come to expect were there in Ambler's book. There was the amateur sleuth, successful mystery writer Charles Latimer, who, in the grand tradition, sees what the police do not and solves the crime.

The story too was relatively straightforward. Latimer is taken by a mysterious Colonel Haki to view a body found floating in the Bosporus. It is that of Dimitrios Makropoulos, an assassin, drug dealer and thief. Haki confesses to knowing little that is concrete about Dimitrios other than that he is the worst kind of criminal, but declares the case closed. Latimer, stung by Colonel Haki's comment that while Latimer may be a successful mystery writer, he knows nothing about real murder, sets out to unmask Dimitrios, to trace his story back to the beginning. It is a safe enough endeavor; Dimitrios is, after all, dead.

But the setting! Here the sanitized English village was replaced by decadent villas on the Turkish coast, dimly lit back alleys and seedy nightclubs of Sofia, revelations over absinthe (absinthe!) in smoky restaurants in Smyrna, hidden, moldering apartments in pre-war Paris. It was not just that the world through which Latimer, first offended, then titillated and finally obsessed, pursued his goal was exotic, indeed threatening. It was also disturbing, a seething mass of corruption, of dissimilitude, of betrayal of the worst kind. These were places not just to be viewed, but to be experienced in all their puzzling complexity.

As a writer of mysteries now myself, I have come to appreciate Ambler's absolute control over the universe he created, the tantalizingly slow manner in which Dimitrios is revealed, the mounting sense of foreboding as Latimer, cocooned in his essential Englishness, blind to the clues around him, continues his inquiries. Rereading this book recently reminded me how much I was affected by it. The mysteries I write are all set in exotic climes with a protagonist who, like Latimer a stranger in a strange land, must understand the place in which she finds herself, as well as the people, to unravel the web of deceit at the heart of the story.

From the way Ambler so seamlessly integrates setting and the huge social changes sweeping Europe in the pre-World War II period into his story, I learned that setting should never be a backdrop, but in almost every respect a living, breathing character to which both author and reader must pay heed. I learned that in mysteries, as in life, a certain amount of ambiguity must be tolerated, that the universe does not always unfold as it should. For in Ambler's book, while it seems it is our hero, the intelligent and inventive Charles Latimer who triumphs, in reality it is the pervasive corruption, the social evils spurred by vested economic interests, the rot at the core of society that Dimitrios represents and that are so aptly mirrored in the decaying world through which Latimer travels, that, undiminished, hold sway.

Lyn Hamilton writes an archaeological mystery series featuring antique dealer Lara McClintoch who travels the world in search of the rare and beautiful, finding more than a little murder and mayhem along the way. The most recent novel in her series is *The Moai Murders*, set on Easter Island.

William Kent Krueger on
The Big Sleep by Raymond Chandler (1939)

Raymond Chandler saved my life.

Or that's how it felt to me at eighteen.

I was a senior in high school, a lonely kid who'd just moved to Manteca, a small town in California. (Think Petticoat Junction with pretensions.) The school was decent, with a faculty intent on channeling all graduates into college. In 1968, with the Vietnam War chewing up legions of young men, this probably showed more intelligence and humanity than I gave credit for back then.

At school I was steeped in the classics. *Pride and Prejudice.* Shakespeare. *The Federalist Papers.* On my own, I'd read a few books that I knew were considered classics, notably Salinger's painful *Catcher in the Rye*. But the truth was that I was foundering in a sea of archaic prose and drowning in "meaning."

One night after a football game and the dance that followed, I came home to find my father watching an old movie on television. I recognized Bogart. The movie was *The Big Sleep.* I settled in beside him, shared his popcorn and the flick. Somewhere along the way my father, who taught literature at my high school, confided to me in a voice that suggested he was letting me see dirty French postcards, "It's based on a mystery novel. A guy named Raymond Chandler. Junk."

All right, he might not have said *junk* but that was the implication.

I checked the book out of the public library the next day and discovered a territory of dark classics that neither my father nor any teacher I knew appreciated.

The Big Sleep spoke directly to me, from the casual self-deprecation of the opening — "I was neat, clean, shaved and sober, and I didn't care who knew it." — to the tough and beautiful epiphany near the end:

What did it matter where you lay once you were dead? In a dirty sump or in a marble tower on top of a high hill? You were dead, you were sleeping the big sleep, you were not bothered by things like that. Oil and water were the same as wind and air to you. You just slept the big sleep, not caring about the nastiness of how you died or where you fell.

I read it as a poetic rail against the callous misuse of wealth and power, and also a tribute to the noble disheveled figure who walked the dark, lonely streets battling on behalf of the small truths and the disenfranchised. That's how it seemed to me, a senior in high school faced with a senseless power structure eager to send me off to die in a war I didn't understand or believe in. I was thrilled with Marlowe, the kind of guy who faced that kind of mindless authority with a cigarette wedged in his lips and a cutting remark ready on his tongue. I loved his style.

I didn't read Chandler because he wrote in a genre. I didn't even know the genre existed. I read him because of what he said to me. In a way, his Marlowe seemed to be what Salinger's Holden Caulfield dreamed of becoming. He was the figure all alone in the rye field whose duty it was to keep the innocent from falling off the edge. I wanted to be that figure, too.

The Big Sleep introduced me to Chandler's work, to his stunning metaphors and similes, to his threadbare vision of chivalry, to his noir California that was not Manteca. It could easily have been any of his other books, however, all of which I consumed in short order.

I don't write like Chandler. No one does, really. I return to him, though, whenever I'm tired and beat down, whenever going on seems useless. Marlowe felt that way a few times, too. Somehow he always found the strength to enter the shadows of those dark LA streets and do the tough job. I still love his style.

William Kent Krueger writes the Cork O'Connor mystery series set in the great Northwoods of Minnesota. His work has received a number of awards including the Anthony Award for Best Novel of 2004 for *Blood Hollow*. His most recent novel is *Mercy Falls*.

Tony Perona on
And Then There Were None by Agatha Christie (1939)

Agatha Christie killed me off.

That was my introduction to the Queen of Crime, and it wasn't pretty. I was the final victim, the last of the *Ten Little Indians* to die in the theater version of the novel known today as *And Then There Were None*. I don't remember much else about that summer season of theater at Speedway High School (although I'm certain my portrayal of William Henry Blore was brilliant), but that play still stands out in my mind as an excellent piece of writing. It's a cleverly conceived mystery, and I love how the clues to its solution are carefully scattered among each character's demise.

Just a few years later I received two more exposures to Christie that helped me understand why she was so highly regarded among mystery aficionados. Those two were the elegant 1974 film version of *Murder on the Orient Express* and the final Hercule Poirot novel *Curtain*, published in 1975. I enjoyed *Murder on the Orient Express* so much I saw it many times. I picked up *Curtain* because it was a major bestseller and because Christie had recently died. In fact, *Curtain* was still riding the bestseller lists the week her obituary was published.

What I admired about Christie then, and still do today, is that there was no puzzle, no variation of the murder mystery, that she was not willing to tackle or create. From the apparent solution of "nobody did it" in *And Then There Were None* to the "everybody did it" of *Murder on the Orient Express* to the "he had to die to prove it" solution of *Curtain*, Christie proved she could master them all. She set the bar incredibly high for any mystery writer who followed.

It was natural, then, that I looked to Christie's works as an example and an inspiration some twenty years later when I decided to try my hand at a murder mystery. I was intrigued by the closed room aspect of Indian Island in *And Then There Were None*, and so I set my first mystery, *Second Advent*, in the small town of Clinton, Indiana. Although not as isolated as Indian Island, the town was small enough to provide my sleuth, Nick Bertetto, with a limited number of suspects. As learned from Hercule Poirot and Miss Marple, Nick approaches each suspect and asks piercing questions, trying to determine the facts. Who had motive? Who had opportunity? And most important, who is lying? Catching the crook in his or her lie is an essential part of solving the crime.

I also love Christie's tradition of amateur sleuths. Nick is really no different from Miss Marple or the esteemed television mystery maven Jessica Fletcher, who owes more than a little of her inspiration to Miss Marple. Nick is not opposed to incorporating such techniques as eavesdropping or encouraging gossip in his dogged investigation to figure out whodunit. He will even place himself in danger if that's what it takes to solve the mystery. And it often does. It's one of the things Christie taught us about amateur sleuths.

So I owe much to Christie. My becoming a published author was made possible only by the fact that, when I was in high school, she dropped a big block of white marble on top of my head, crushing the life out of me.

Agatha, it hurt so good.

Tony Perona is a former General Motors advertising/public relations manager who became the first man to take the corporation's two-year leave-of-absence to care for his children. He writes about Nick Bertetto, a stay-at-home dad and former investigative reporter, whose mysteries involve a supernatural element. The latest is *Angels Whisper*.

Nancy Pickard on
Double Indemnity by James M. Cain (1944)

At first blush, which is something a hardboiled writer would never do, James M. Cain does not look like an authorial influence on me. He's not just hardboiled, he's one of the fathers of the hardboiled genre, while I am usually placed among the cozies. What in the world could he and I have in common?

That he is a big influence on me is something I can never deny, even if nobody else ever believes it. Look at the name of my first mystery heroine: Jenny Cain. What's her dad's name? Jimmy Cain. I didn't even realize I had lifted James M. Cain's name until many books into my Jenny Cain series. That theft was unconscious on my part — honest, officer — but certain other assets of the original Mr. Cain I will happily confess to stealing.

The man loved melodrama. So do I, and when I start to hesitate before committing a fictional act of it, I think: What would James do? I know what the answer is: he'd go for the heat, he'd go over the top, because that's the kind of writer he was, a melodramatic one, thank god. He married hot characters to cold, spare dialogue. It is that strange and wonderful juxtaposition that gives *Double Indemnity*, and his other work, so much of its dramatic tension and irony.

The man loved to play against his readers' biases and expectations, and so do I. In *Double Indemnity*, the readers of his day expected a man to be the smart and canny one, the player. Cain obviously knew that, and so he lured readers down the path of their own sexism, and then he pulled the rug out from under them at the same time that he pulled it out from under his male character.

He loved to surprise readers and his characters in as many other ways as possible, too. I happen to think that the best mystery and suspense writers are those who understand how very much readers adore surprises. Surprise me, we are begging every book we pick up, even when we pick up a book in a mystery series that we think we're reading only for the comfort of its familiarity. Somehow, somewhere in this book, surprise me. If the author doesn't — and most don't — we are disappointed, even in our favorites. For first-time readers of *Double Indemnity*, reading it sometime in the first twenty or so years of its existence, there was one delicious surprise after another.

This will probably sound like heresy to his fans, but the writer I privately align him with is none other than Agatha Christie. Partly, it's that they were, in their individual corners of the mystery world, masters of limning characters with quick strokes. Nobody did that better in their time than the two of them. But I also see in both of them that love of melodrama (consider Christie's final scenes in which All Is Revealed), that love of playing against their readers' prejudices, and their love of surprise.

Double Indemnity is a little masterpiece of getting a story told quicky and urgently and making you blink, if not gasp, with surprise. It is hot and cold, sentimental and cynical. My breath comes more quickly whenever I think of it, even now, all these years and novels later.

The ability to leave readers breathless is a fine quality in a writer, and nobody ever did it any better than James M. Cain in *Double Indemnity*.

Nancy Pickard has written sixteen mystery novels and dozens of short stories. She has won three Agatha Awards, two Macavity Awards, two Anthony Awards and a Shamus Award. She is a three-time Edgar Award nominee. Her latest books are *Seven Steps on the Writer's Path*, co-written with Lynn Lott, and *The Virgin of Small Plains*.

Carole Nelson Douglas on
Miss Pym Disposes by Josephine Tey (1946)

A 1950s edition of *Three by Tey*, including *Miss Pym Disposes*, sits on the highest shelf of my bookcase next to Dorothy L. Sayers' Peter Wimsey novels. "Josephine Tey" was Elizabeth MacIntosh, who wrote eight unique mysteries. *The Daughter of Time*, in which her bedridden Inspector Alan Grant clears Richard III of villainy, makes the top mystery lists. Yet Tey was so much more than Grant, a continuing but often peripheral figure in her works, not the keystone Sayers made of Wimsey.

Why does *Miss Pym Disposes* abide in Olympian isolation with Sayers' *Gaudy Night*? As a women's college graduate, I'm drawn to female academia: Sayers' Oxford that nourished the professorial nuns of my much-later college days (my creative writing instructor baby-sat J.R.R. Tolkien's children!) and Tey's girls' College of Physical Education. Sayers hunted for twisted psychology among her nun-like lady dons. Tey focused on a hardy group of spirited, or dispirited, young women.

Much shorter than *Gaudy Night*, *Miss Pym Disposes* achieves the neat trick of quickly introducing a clear and compelling cast of a dozen students and a half-dozen teachers, all seen from the viewpoint of a visitor connected to the college. Unlike Harriet Vane, who is contemplating whether a woman can have an independent intellectual, emotional and physical relationship with any man, specifically the brilliantly complex Wimsey, "little" Miss Pym is the female equivalent of a contented English bachelor. Precise and dainty, with a certain timidity beneath her self-possession, Miss Pym has authored a freakishly famous pop psychology book that makes her a sought-after "expert" lecturer. (Tantalizing references indicate some modest courting encounters with an "Alan" whose minor male domestic habits do not quite win over Miss Pym.)

Observing the girls, she witnesses a terrible injustice when the headmistress hands the plum post-graduation job to a flawed and unlikable candidate instead of the "star" student. Everyone opposes this decision, even newcomer Miss Pym, who saw the unworthy Rouse cheating during an examination. When Rouse is found unconscious in a solo gym accident, Innes, the deserving girl, gets the post by default.

Twice Miss Pym faces dilemmas in the novel. While monitoring a test session, she observes Rouse acting oddly and later finds a tiny crib book. She stopped the cheating so she throws the book away, which she regrets later. Miss Pym also was near the gym during Rouse's solitary session. Finding footprints and a shoe ornament, she realizes that the accident was deliberate When Rouse dies, one of the girls with their lives ahead of them faces the gallows, likely the brilliant but not always sympathetic Innes.

As in the adage "man proposes and God disposes" — and like many an amateur sleuth — Miss Pym is tempted to play God and to temper justice with mercy. Disablement, not death was intended. Pym forces a repentant Innes to relinquish the post, dedicating her life to the injured and ill in a suffocating backwater.

But God disposes in even more mysterious ways than Miss Pym suspects. She discovers that Innes repented not because she's the attacker, but because the injury was done by another on her unknowing behalf. Miss Pym has punished the wrong girl, and the amoral perpetrator goes free to a life of privilege and untroubled conscience.

Tey's novels are razor-sharp psychological studies, neither thrillers nor cozies. They seek the skull beneath the grin. Tey herself is a master of witty tone and skewering social observation, which is why this book has clung to my literary ribs for decades. *Miss Pym Disposes* investigates the risks and hubris of presuming others' motives and deeds, of playing God, as all writers do. It's why I love writing and reading about ethically challenged characters, even and especially when they make, and must live with, ghastly mistakes.

Carole Nelson Douglas has authored 50 novels in five genres. She wrote the first Sherlockian novel starring a woman, American diva and Holmes outwitter Irene Adler, most recently seen in *Spider Dance*. The Midnight Louie mysteries feature a Runyonesque feline sleuth and four human crime solvers; *Cat in a Quicksilver Caper* arrived in spring 2006.

Hazel Holt on
The Franchise Affair by Josephine Tey (1948)

There are certain books that, when you first read them, give an instant glow of pleasure and then remain to resonate in the mind. You never forget them. *The Franchise Affair* by Josephine Tey is like that. Although it was written in 1948, it is still fresh and true today. This is because, like all great mystery novels, the plot is derived from the characters, and Tey's characters are real and three-dimensional.

The plot may seem slight. A middle-aged woman, Marion Sharpe, and her mother are accused by a schoolgirl of kidnapping and beating her. And that's it. No murder, none of the more brutal crimes that feature in most mystery novels, but Tey makes this apparently simple story complex and fascinating.

Although there is police involvement, the investigation is undertaken (reluctantly at first) by a local lawyer, Robert Blair, whose life gradually becomes irretrievably entwined with those of Marion and her mother.

The characters of the two women (both eccentric and unusual) are presented so sympathetically that it is obvious to the reader that the girl is lying, so it is not a question of whodunit, but simply of why and how. The slow unfolding of the story, the unraveling of the mystery, the stripping away of layers of deceit are all so finely done, the pieces of the jigsaw so neatly slotted into place that the final solution is completely satisfying.

The book begins with Robert Blair sitting in his office "in the lazy atmosphere of a spring evening in a little market town, where the last post goes out at 3:45 [and] the day loses whatever momentum it ever had long before four o'clock." But Milford, with its elegant Georgian buildings and its air of quiet tranquility, and the schoolgirl, with her young candid face, are not what they seem. Other novels by Josephine Tey, *Brat Farrar* and *Miss Pym Disposes* which mark her as one of the finest exponents of her art, are also about what lies beneath the surface, what is real and what is false.

In *The Franchise Affair,* the surface is smooth and pleasant but gradually the dark side begins to appear. In 1948, the war was not long over, there were still bomb sites in London and things were moving under the surface of the social life of even a small country town. Gossip now could be whipped up by a manipulative tabloid press, leading to mob violence and menace. There is a hint here of genuine evil, mirrored in the cold, calculating deceit of the girl. It is a passionate desire for the truth to be known that informs Robert Blair's investigation. It is not enough that the women should simply "get off," their names must be completely cleared. This appears to be achieved, but it is significant, though, and typical of Josephine Tey's honesty, that although this is achieved they still have to leave not just the town but the country, to go to the New World, to Canada, to start their lives afresh, free of the taint of rumour.

The writing is crisp and elegant. The dialogue reads perfectly, as might be expected of a fine dramatist (as Gordon Daviot, she wrote the brilliant *Richard of Bordeaux*) who hears the words spoken in her head before she writes. The final denouement in the court scene is a splendid piece of theatre. But she doesn't end on this high note. More subtly she gives us a dying fall that eases us gently into the obliquely satisfying happy ending.

After working for many years as an editor, reviewer and feature writer, **Hazel Holt** published her first mystery book (*Mrs. Malory Investigates*) at the age of 60. Since then Hazel has published one book a year in her Mrs. Malory series, the latest being *No Cure For Death* (Signet, 2005).

Carolyn Wheat on
Cat of Many Tails by Ellery Queen (1949)

Surely the title should have been *Cat of Nine Tails*. After all, nine people were murdered by the serial killer known as the Cat, who terrorized Manhattan during one hot summer much as the Son of Sam would do in real life years later. Fred Dannay and Manfred B. Lee, writing as Ellery Queen, captured the rising hysteria of a city gone mad with terror as it waited for the next victim to turn up in Central Park or a subway station. When detective Ellery Queen realized that the victims, who were wholly unrelated to one another, had been murdered in descending order of age, the panic really hit the tabloid fan.

The portrait of New York City under pressure from intense heat and growing fear is only one of the reasons *Cat of Many Tails* has stuck with me for so many years. Even more important to me as a writer is what the case does to Ellery. This Ellery is far different from the condescending thinking machine who made his debut in 1929; this Ellery takes every murder personally. He begins the book in a state of depression triggered by the Van Horn case (*Ten Days' Wonder*). "He had found himself betrayed by his own logic. The old blade had turned suddenly in his hand; he had aimed at the guilty with it and it had run through the innocent."

When he comes out of his self-imposed exile to take the case, he not only matches wits with the Cat, he dedicates every waking moment to capturing the killer before more innocents die. He plunges into despair as he fails to prevent more murders. Nine people are dead when Ellery finally unmasks the Cat — but his victory turns hollow when he discovers the truth behind the truth. Once again his logic skewered the innocent and let the guilty go free.

The conclusion of this extraordinary case brings Ellery to the point of despair all over again. For "the logical successor to Sherlock Holmes" to doubt his sanity calls the entire detective enterprise into question. If the killer uses the subtlety of Queen's intelligence against him, if he can turn that fabled intellect against itself, then can any detective dare to match wits with a killer ever again? Is the detective playing God?

This sounds a lot more portentous than it reads on the page. The book is a wonderful glimpse into New York City at the close of the 1940s, and it even has a few things to say about race relations, which is highly unusual in books of the period. Skip the obligatory romantic comedy and keep your eye on Ellery's manic-depressive mood swings as he wrestles with the puzzle of the Cat killings. We take it for granted today that the detective has personal feelings, but at the time Cat was written, this was not a given. Murder takes its toll and in *Cat of Many Tails*, Ellery Queen the writer gave us a portrait of Ellery Queen the detective that showed the high price he paid for his brilliance.

Did he fail again, as he had in the Van Horn case? Up to a point, yes. Does that mean he will stop using his remarkable brain in the service of justice? As a world-famous psychiatrist tells him, "You have failed before; you will fail again. That is the nature and the role of man." The great man reminds Ellery "There is but one God, and there is no other but He."

Carolyn Wheat has won the Agatha, Anthony, Macavity and Shamus Awards for her short stories. Two of her six Cass Jameson legal mysteries were nominated for the Edgar Award. Her book *How To Write Killer Fiction* has been called a "must for every writer's bookshelf." Her current project: *Everything I Know About Storytelling I Learned From Star Trek*. She also teaches writing at the University of San Diego Extension.

Carola Dunn on
Brat Farrar by Josephine Tey (1949)

As a teenager, I always had my nose in a book. Come to that, I was a bookworm as a child and things haven't changed much since. But one of the few non-literary books, and the only mystery, that made a still-memorable impression on my teenage self was Josephine Tey's *Brat Farrar*.

Why? For a start, it has an unusual plot. The protagonist is a con man, an impersonator with fraudulent intentions. The possibility that a murder has occurred, several years in the past, doesn't come out till the latter half of the book.

I've never felt any particular urgency about killing my victims quickly. I like to get to know the characters before their lives are disrupted by murder. However, I don't think *Brat Farrar* in particular influenced me in this respect. Many older traditional whodunits work this way. It gives the reader a chance to see how the cast, including major suspects, behave in the normal way, and to watch their interactions as they move towards a sudden death. I find it more interesting trying to work out who is the murderer when I already know the people involved.

However, *Brat Farrar* is by no means a traditional whodunit. Most of my mysteries are, except for a couple, *Damsel in Distress* and *The Case of the Murdered Muckraker*, neither of which has anything in common with the plot of *Brat Farrar*. The former is a story of a kidnapping and the latter is a cross-country chase — in a biplane — after the person Daisy believes to be the murderer.

Another difference is that *Brat Farrar* is not part of a series. In all my mysteries, my main protagonist is Daisy Dalrymple, with Detective Chief Inspector Alec Fletcher of Scotland Yard providing an alternative perspective. People who read the whole series in order get to know Daisy and Alec very well, yet in each book I have to allow for those who haven't read any other titles. I have to introduce the pair to new readers without repeating myself to such an extent that it bores those who are familiar with them. This is only possible because Daisy is a person readers like to spend time with. Since I spend more time with Daisy than anyone else does, it's important to me, too.

In *Brat Farrar*, by the time murder comes into the picture, the readers' sympathies have been captured for both the impersonator and the family he's trying to con. "Brat," the eponymous protagonist, may be a crook, but he's basically a nice person succumbing after a struggle to irresistible temptation. The Ashbys are introduced as pleasant, well-meaning people, the day-to-day course of their lives upset only by the intrusion of Brat, pretending to be a long lost member of the family.

Unlike her *Miss Pym Disposes*, where most of the cast — including the protagonist — are pretty unlikable, in *Brat Farrar*, Tey develops her characters with warmth and humanity. I like them. I care what happens to them. And this is where

Brat Farrar influenced my writing. After reading lots of Agatha Christie, where the puzzles may be great but on the whole the characters range from not very interesting to positively irritating (I include Miss Marple and Poirot among the latter), it was wonderfully refreshing and inspiring to come across a mystery full of people I wanted to know.

So all those readers who write to me saying they regard Daisy as a good friend can ultimately thank Josephine Tey.

Carola Dunn (www.geocities.com/CarolaDunn) writes the Daisy Dalrymple series, set in 1920s England. The series was nominated for the Romantic Times Lifetime Achievement award. The fifteenth, *Gunpowder Plot*, will appear in 2006. Dunn is also author of over 30 Regencies. Born in England, she lives in Oregon.

K.j.a Wishnia on
Trouble is My Business by Raymond Chandler (1950)

Oh, no. Not another male author of hardboiled literature writing a paean to "Saint" Raymond. But this was more than 30 years ago, I was still a kid and the reading assignments in school bored the crap out of me. (No seventh grader should ever be required to read *The Light in the Forest*.) I had no trouble reading horror, fantasy and mystery on my own, and by eighth grade, I had read all of Sherlock Holmes.

Then one day I picked up a 95¢ Ballantine paperback of four stories by some guy named Raymond Chandler. The extract on the back cover grabbed me immediately. Chandler's hyperbolic descriptions were way beyond the bland stuff we got in school. This femme fatale's hair was "a dusky red, like a fire under control but still dangerous," and her eyes were "lapis-lazuli blue," whatever that meant.

It wasn't just that the detective, Philip Marlowe, had a snappy comeback for every wiseass remark thrown his way (and there were plenty of those). These stories showed me a world where a basically decent guy was surrounded by phony glitz and manipulative double-dealers who were, with rare — even idealized — exceptions, only in it for themselves. Even though I was in junior high school, I understood and admired Marlowe. He was a man of his word, surviving on 25 bucks a day plus expenses, whose investigation might take him to a ritzy apartment building with a lobby "not quite as big as Yankee Stadium," where he was too shabby to be announced by the snooty concierge, yet the supposedly high-class layout was lousy with swindlers and gun-toting bodyguards.

But Chandler always took it further than that. Hardboiled isn't about how many drinks you down, how many dames you tangle with, how many doors you kick in. It's an attitude that the world is hopelessly corrupt, and solving a crime or two isn't going to change a damn thing about it. (This was the year Nixon resigned, which probably helped.) After all, the tough dame with the smoky-red hair explains that she's in this caper because a millionaire ruined her father, with a fountain pen instead of a .38, and a mobster admits, "You can't convict a couple million bucks of murder in this man's town."

These stories set the stage for Chandler's classic novels. "Goldfish" refers to the system-wide corruption during Prohibition, when a local tells Marlowe how he used to unload "Canadian hooch" while the Coast Guard stood by watching. This outlook was nothing like the clear-cut moral universe of Sherlock Holmes, and Marlowe's response to it is a pathological sarcasm that provided me with a survival guide to life.

I loved the world of Sherlock Holmes, where the great detective could identify a man's point of origin from a quick glance at the mud spattered on his shoes. But I lived in the hardboiled world of an America that had no God except money, where some cops were just as likely to beat the hell out of you as to help you find your car keys.

I learned early on not to imitate Chandler, because all you end up with is imitation Chandler. But the attitude stayed with me: the idea that we are surrounded by falsehood, in a place where the glitter is all tinsel, and where muscle and money almost always win, with money often trumping muscle.

But it is also a place where the detective still goes out to face the music and do what must be done. That's my kind of hero. And still is.

K.j.a. Wishnia's (wishnik@sunysuffolk.edu) first novel, *23 Shades of Black*, was nominated for the Edgar and the Anthony Awards. Other titles in the Filomena Buscarsela series include *Soft Money* and *Red House*, which made best mystery of the year lists at Library Journal and The Washington Post, respectively.

Jeffrey Marks on
A Murder is Announced by Agatha Christie (1950)

In the summer of my sixteenth year, I discovered Agatha Christie. I had been a voracious reader since I had learned to read, and had already managed to win awards for my work. Yet the works of Agatha Christie so lured me and captivated me that I knew I wanted to write mysteries.

A Murder is Announced was written in 1950, near the end of Christie's most prolific and creative period. The plot, for those who have not had the pleasure, is convoluted. An advertisement in the village paper announces a murder to occur that very evening. At the appointed hour, neighbors arrive with excuses. The lights go off and shots are fired. The hostess for the evening is wounded, but the shooter dies in the aftermath of the attack.

Soon after, Miss Marple arrives in town and tries to get to the heart of the matter. She learns that the hostess is the heiress to millions, and if she dies before the millionaire financier, then the estate goes to the children of his ne'er-do-well sister. The children disappeared during the confusion of World War II and could be close by. Miss Marple solves the case after two more gruesome deaths, meant to cover the the tracks of a wily murderer.

This book has served as a muse for me because it encompasses so much of what I enjoy in a cozy mystery. Despite the detractors who claim her characters to be cardboard, Christie showed her skills at capturing human nature in the book. Her portrait of the sister who had been trapped in a life of want and despair because of her affliction and her father's attitude is well-drawn, even though the reader never meets the girl. The devotion of two romantic couples is also well portrayed as they struggle with finances and the aftermath of the war.

One of Christie's most enduring themes is that the past has long shadows. Lettie's past career is the impetus for the crimes. So many times in Christie's work, small details from history come back to haunt the characters, and this is well portrayed in this book.

A Murder is Announced intrigued me from the time I read its title. Of course, a murder is announced; it's a mystery novel. Yet the foreshadowing done by the title only heightens the tension as the allotted time for the murder nears. Likewise, the cake "Delicious Death" can only spell poisoning for an unsuspecting character, and indeed it does late in the book. Even though Christie gives the reader these hints of what will come, it does nothing to hurt the pacing or suspense.

Finally, Christie manages to add social commentary to a solid mystery. Christie's eye for the times is shown throughout the book. Her depiction of a lesbian couple is one of the earliest representations of same-sex couples. Such a couple would never have appeared in fiction before the war. Additionally, Christie paints a picture of the time. *A Murder is Announced*, with its subplots of people who are not who they seem, could only have been written in the days after the war when the English population was in flux, having moved repeatedly due to bombing and evacuations. The minor food black market allowed the suspects easy access to each other's homes.

Christie managed to fit all of these elements into 200-odd pages. As I reread this deceptively complex book, it continues to serve as a reminder of what I would like to accomplish with my own novels. A worthy goal.

Jeffrey Marks is the Edgar, Agatha, Anthony, Macavity and Maxwell nominated author of the History of Mystery series that includes *Who Was That Lady?* and *Atomic Renaissance*. He is also the author of a series set in current day Cincinnati, starting with *The Scent of Murder*.

Peter Lovesey on
Strangers on a Train by Patricia Highsmith (1950)

She once came to a Detection Club dinner and I wish I could say I spoke to her. I didn't because I was shy and she had a dark, brooding look that matched her books and didn't encourage an approach. If I'd had the nerve I would have told Patricia Highsmith that reading one of her books was my Damascus Road experience. My crime-writing career had got under way with a series of historical whodunits that fitted the conventional detective story. After eight books I was lucky enough to get a TV series called *Sergeant Cribb*. You might think this would guarantee an unending stream of Cribb stories. In fact it stopped me in my tracks. My store of ideas for future books was all used up providing new TV scripts. And I found that the actors who played Cribb and his sidekick Thackeray got into my head. No longer could I see the characters I'd created. Time for a change, I thought, time to break with the whodunit form.

Strangers on a Train was Patricia Highsmith's first novel, surely the most accomplished debut by a crime writer in the twentieth century. The title is the plot. The menace is there in the first sentence: "The train tore along with an angry, irregular rhythm." Two would-be murderers meet by chance on the train and agree to swap victims. The crimes will be untraceable, the premise for a novel of exquisite suspense involving themes of guilt, obsession and complicity. The basic plot was apparently first used by Baroness Orczy in one of her "Old Man in the Corner" stories. Whether Highsmith had read the Orczy version is uncertain and unimportant. She turned a clever story device into a major artistic achievement with her intensity of character and subtlety of language. That astute film director, Alfred Hitchcock, saw the potential, bought the rights and made the movie within a year.

I came to the book at some time in the '70s, and the appeal of writing a murder from the point of view of the criminal excited me. I read other titles by Highsmith, notably the series featuring the engaging killer Tom Ripley. This inverted form of crime writing would be fascinating to try. I was moved first to write *The False Inspector Dew*, about a 1920s dentist who works out a way to kill and dispose of his wife on an ocean liner. Breaking the mould of the whodunit was a big step forward for me. The story won the Gold Dagger and was bought by Columbia for a movie — one of those movies that was never made.

Since then, I've returned at intervals to this kind of story. The challenge is to persuade the reader to identify with a killer. *On the Edge*, with more than a nod to *Strangers on a Train*, was about two women who murder their husbands in post-war England. In *The Reaper,* I set myself a bigger challenge: to

105

make a vicar carry out several murders. It was amoral, and I'm glad to say I have a sheaf of letters from members of the clergy saying how much they enjoyed it.

So I have a lot to thank Patricia Highsmith for. And, incidentally, her book *Plotting and Writing Suspense Fiction* (1966) ranks with Stephen King's *On Writing* as one of the most useful books any mystery writer could pick up.

Peter Lovesey's mysteries have won awards across the world and been translated into 33 languages. He started out with Victorian settings but his recent books have been set in modern Bath and feature the police detective Peter Diamond. His latest, *The Circle* (2005), is about murders among a group of writers.

Susan Oleksiw on
They Came to Baghdad by Agatha Christie (1951)

In 1975 I was swimming against the tide of politics and family in trying to extricate myself from graduate school for a year of living in India. I had a grant and a program. What I did not have was support. The Government of India was giving foreign scholars a hard time about visas and study programs, and my family didn't see the urgency. In this setting I read Agatha Christie's *They Came to Baghdad*.

I do not know how this title came into my hands. My dissertation professor noticed it in my stack of books one morning and remarked he had read Christie in the Netherlands to help perfect his English. He said nothing about whether or not he enjoyed her work, but that was the beginning of my love of crime fiction.

Victoria Jones, a young English woman in her twenties, is a dismal typist condemned to temp jobs in London. Just after being fired from one she meets a charming young man in a park, and they immediately hit it off. But, sadly, he is on his way to

Baghdad to work for one of the British Empire's typical oddities, a man spreading good will by sharing Shakespeare with the world. When Edward and Victoria separate, she can think only of following him, but how? Luckily, an opportunity to accompany an American woman, Mrs. Hamilton Clipp, arises, and Victoria is on her way.

Victoria brings Mrs. Clipp safely to Baghdad, and once there is left nearly penniless and entirely on her own. But Victoria is one of those irrepressible heroines whose guile and intrepidness see them through. She tracks down Edward at the library he works for, The Olive Branch, but he's not there, so she volunteers to help until he returns.

Also on their way to Baghdad are numerous agents of governments and shadowy forces intent on disrupting an important conference. An American woman disappears on her way to Baghdad; a secret agent sidesteps danger on his desperate flight; and a flamboyant world-renowned traveler opts for a hotel rather than more official quarters. One of them ends up dying in Victoria's bed. Our heroine is tossed into a dangerous world never imagined in any of her fantasies.

The ease with which Victoria Jones sets off for the Middle East reflects a trip Christie herself took in 1928 soon after her divorce from her first husband, an act of independence and confidence as rare in 1950 as it was in 1928. Along with the usual cast of foreigners found in eastern capitals, Christie opens a window into the world of archaeology and scholars working under the purest of circumstances — without the distractions of urban life and the comforts of civilization. It is here that Victoria, as an individual, comes into her own. She begins her adventure as a somewhat silly girl and emerges as a smart, astute, and dangerously competent young woman.

Christie may be admired most for titles such as *The Murder of Roger Akroyd* or *Murder on the Orient Express*, but her lesser-known mysteries are just as strong. She absorbed other cultures whole and understood the subtle ways in which the East and West blended and clashed. She used it all to tell a good story, and give us a look into the kind of character she admired.

Susan Oleksiw is the author of the Mellingham series; the latest is *A Murderous Innocence* (Five Star, 2006). A second series character, Hindu-American photographer Anita Ray, who investigates murders in South India, appears in short stories. Oleksiw's first publication was *A Reader's Guide to the Classic British Mystery* (1988).

Bill Crider on
The Big Kill by Mickey Spillane (1951)

Anthony Boucher, one of the finest critics ever to write about the mystery, called one of Mickey Spillane's novels such "a glorification of force, cruelty, and extra-legal methods that the novel might be made required reading in a Gestapo training school."

So is it possible that my not-quite-hardboiled Sheriff Dan Rhodes series could be in some way descended from a book like that? In a word, yes. Here's how:

I first encountered Spillane's novels about Mike Hammer in high school when a friend came by my house one night with a copy of *Kiss Me, Deadly*. He proceeded to read aloud the passage early in the novel when Hammer, having picked up a beautiful hitchhiker, is stopped at a roadblock. When Hammer is asked if he's seen anyone along the road, the hitcher takes his hand and puts it inside her long trench coat, where Hammer feels nothing but her smooth, bare thigh. My friend and I didn't know much about the art of literature, but we knew what we liked, and this was it.

After that introduction I naturally went on to read other

Spillane books, but it was several years later, when I was in my early twenties, that I ran across *The Big Kill*. I grabbed it as soon as I saw it, and for some reason (maybe I had latent fascist tendencies), I liked it even more than the other Spillane novels that I'd read. Here's a sample of the prose: "I snapped the side of the rod across his jaw and laid the flesh open to the bone. He dropped the sap and staggered into the big boy with a scream starting to come up out of his throat only to get it cut off in the middle as I pounded his teeth back into his mouth with the end of the barrel."

I wished I could write like that.

So I gave it a try. I sat down at my little portable Olivetti (ask your parents) and knocked out three chapters and an outline about a tough private eye who was a lot like Mike Hammer but who operated in Austin, Texas, instead of New York City. Mercifully, all I remember about the proposed masterpiece is that there was an attempt on the PI's life by a perfume-wearing hit man in the first chapter and that the PI throws him off the University of Texas Tower (27 stories high) in the third chapter.

By that time of my life, I'd read a great many Gold Medal novels, most of which seemed to have been influenced by Spillane, and I thought that Gold Medal would be the perfect place to send my proposal. I was certain that I was on my way to fame, fortune, and bestsellerdom.

It didn't work out quite like that, of course. Some short-sighted editor at Gold Medal rejected my brilliant work, and I gave up on writing for many years, if you don't count all the research papers I produced in graduate school and the poetry I wrote for a while after that.

Eventually I started writing mystery fiction again, and the first result was a Nick Carter novel called *The Coyote Connection*, written in collaboration with a friend named Jack Davis. The Spillane influence is obvious, I think, in the chapter devoted to agricultural torture.

109

A few years later, I discovered my own voice in the first Sheriff Dan Rhodes novel, *Too Late to Die*. It's about as far from Spillane as you can get, but the series is still running, nearly twenty years after the first book was published. Go figure.

Bill Crider's first Sheriff Dan Rhodes book, *Too Late to Die*, won the Anthony Award for Best First Mystery Novel in 1986. He and his wife, Judy, are the authors of the 2002 Anthony Award winning short story "Chocolate Moose." The latest novel in the Sheriff Rhodes series is *A Mammoth Murder* (St. Martin's, 2006).

Candace Robb on
The Daughter of Time by Josephine Tey (1951)

The Daughter of Time is required text for historical novelists. No joke. With my latest reading of Josephine Tey's classic crime novel, I see how profoundly the book has influenced my research methods. I've internalized Alan Grant's process, his Yard training.

For those who have not yet read the book, Tey's Scotland Yard inspector Alan Grant is convalescing in hospital. To entertain him, a friend presents him with a stack of portraits of historical figures about whom there is some mystery, encouraging Grant to exercise his gift in reading faces on these portraits. He chooses one and is mortified to discover that the man he's guessed to be a judge is King Richard III, accused in most school history books of murdering his innocent nephews to secure his position. And so with the aid of a young American researcher Grant launches into an investigation of the crime: "He ... wanted to prove to himself that he was right in his face-reading of the portrait; he ... wanted to blot out the shame of having put a criminal on the bench instead of in the dock."

Since first reading this book I've recreated many historic figures in my mysteries and my analysis of the records from which I've teased out a character has been firmly based on Grant's question "who benefits?" and his rule that "in a police investigation you look for any abnormalities in behaviour among the suspects in a crime...." A break in the pattern.

I read the book again as I was writing *The Lady Chapel*, the second Owen Archer mystery, which I based on an actual lawsuit. On rereading Tey's book I noted in my journal that, as befits a classic, the heart of the tale arrives at precisely the halfway point, when Alan Grant says: "The point is that every single man who was there knows that the story was nonsense, and yet it has never been contradicted. It will never be overtaken now. It is a completely untrue story grown to legend while the men who knew it to be untrue looked on and said nothing."

To which his enthusiastic partner-in-research responds: "...the truth of anything at all doesn't lie in someone's account of it. It lies in all the small facts of the time. An advertisement in a paper. The sale of a house. The price of a ring.... Truth isn't in accounts but in account books."

Again, the question of how people behaved proved far more important than what they later said — or did not say — regarding the betrayals at the heart of my case.

I'm currently deep into research for a novel about Edward III's mistress Alice Perrers. The most famous tale about Alice Perrers is that she plucked the rings off the king on his deathbed when she was alone with him and fled the palace. If Walsingham wanted me to believe that story, he should have included some witnesses sympathetic to his side. Alan Grant would have been laughing with me, and he would have agreed with me that it was much more significant that the king publicly protected her right to go about her business and his unobstructed. This was a public document.

Grant says about historians: "They seem to have no talent for the likeliness of any situation. They see history like a peepshow; with two-dimensional figures against a distant background." This was certainly true of the textbooks imposed on me as a child. But he goes further: "A man who is interested in what makes people tick doesn't write history. He writes novels...." That is the key to good historical fiction — getting to the heart of the people. As he analyzes a particular historian's book Grant thinks: "That charming men of great integrity had committed murder in their day [he] knew only too well.... One could not say: Because Richard possessed this quality and that, therefore he was incapable of murder. But one could say: Because Richard possessed these qualities, therefore he is incapable of this murder."

Josephine Tey set her fictional detective to work on exploding a myth that had become truth. How I wish I'd written this book.

Candace Robb writes the Owen Archer mysteries set in fourteenth century York. She is working on the ninth, *The Guilt of Innocents* (Random House UK, 2007), as well as a standalone novel about the life of King Edward III's mistress, Alice Perrers. Robb's most recent book is the third in a trilogy about Margaret Kerr, a young Scottish woman in the time of Wallace and Bruce, *A Cruel Courtship*.

Stephanie Kane on
The Killer Inside Me by Jim Thompson (1952)

Deputy Sheriff Lou Ford is a small town lawman whose violence and sociopathy are cloaked in a folksiness bordering on cliché. Central City, Texas is anywhere men are men and people mind their own business. Narrated in first person, present tense, Ford's very normalcy attracts us until he mentions "the sickness." *The Killer Inside Me* is a near-claustrophobic immersion in Ford's head.

A good-looking cop whose self-awareness is primal and transparent, Ford makes us nervous from the start. The first to see through him is a bum whom Ford runs out of town by casually putting his cigar out in the man's hand. He much prefers, however, to needle folks like the owner of the local café with his homespun wisdom: "I liked the guy — as much as I like most people, anyway — but he was too good to let go. Polite, intelligent: guys like that are my meat.... I could hear his shoes creak as he squirmed. If there's anything worse than a bore, it's a corny bore. But how can you brush off a nice friendly fellow who'd give you his shirt if you asked for it?"

The hook is set when Ford is dispatched to roust a prostitute, Joyce Lakeland. When Ford finds a gun in Joyce's drawer and says to himself, "I wondered why she'd lived so long," the action takes off. As the sickness takes over, Thompson sinks the hook by simultaneously foreshadowing and dipping into Ford's past: "She'd talk. She'd yell her head off. And people would start thinking, thinking and wondering about that time fifteen years ago...."

Ford's voice is as confiding and unsentimental as the ones in our own heads. His awareness that his "sickness" is something to conceal makes him frighteningly human: Lou may hide behind the mask of a rube, but he never kids himself. His lack of internal conflict makes him even more real. Stuck with him in an increasingly nervous present, without authorial intervention to distract or protect us, it is a reality we cannot escape. The irony of *The Killer Inside Me* is that Lou Ford enters us.

Ford seems to have a capacity to care. His father was a physician, and Lou feels a reassuring calm as he pages through his father's psychiatric literature in his old office where he does calculus problems for the hell of it. His adoptive brother once took a rap for Lou and — what a relief! — this might be a story about revenge. He never roughs up prisoners and he feels affection for a troubled boy he mentored. Ford is human enough to recognize that with each act of violence a part of him is dying.

Alienation and corruption run through the story, exploiting and exploding every cliché: the hayseed lawman, prissy schoolmarm, wise old doc, prostitute with a heart of gold. With "the sickness" inside and his identification with outcasts, Ford epitomizes the alienation in us. He has a conscience, a capacity for redemption that seems to transcend his violence and hooks us more than his sickness, regardless of how it ends.

If the mark of great crime writing is voice, compression is the art of suspense. In bleakly poetic prose, Thompson bores into character and plot, relationships wind and double back, the cluster of events intensifies until the ending explodes and implodes. The ultimate suspense lies in watching every vestige of Lou's humanity extinguish as paranoia takes over and he slides into madness. Trapped in his head, we no longer know what's real and what isn't, until finally he's pitiful and we're still sucked in, to the very last line.

Stephanie Kane writes crime novels and legal thrillers. *Extreme Indifference* and *Seeds of Doubt*, her most recent novels starring dyslexic criminal defense lawyer Jackie Flowers, won the 2004 and 2005 Colorado Authors League Award for Genre Fiction, and the 2004 Colorado Book Award for Mystery.

Mary Anna Evans on
The Caves of Steel by Isaac Asimov (1954)

Some people don't respond well to being told, "It can't be done." The seminal science fiction editor John W. Campbell once said it was impossible to write a book that was both a good mystery and a good science fiction novel. He explained that the detective could produce some bit of technology that would solve his problems for him. In other words, books set in the future couldn't possibly play fair with the reader.

In Isaac Asimov's autobiography, *I. Asimov*, he said he "privately thought that this was a foolish statement, because it was only necessary to set the background at the start and avoid introducing anything new in the remainder of the book. You would then have a science fiction story that was legitimate."

In *The Caves of Steel*, the good doctor wrote that book. The mystery is as finely crafted and as fully realized as its futuristic setting. Reading *The Caves of Steel* is like gazing through a telescope fitted with expertly ground lenses. Look through one end, and you learn something about the world around you. Turn the scope around and look through the other lens, and the world looks different. (Actually it looks very, very small.) Everything you see is still true, but your perception has changed. A good mystery can change your worldview. So can good science fiction. This book is both.

Asimov sets the rules of his future Earth early, and his characters — a human detective and his robotic partner — live by them. Even better, those rules drive the plot. When the detective makes a deduction that proves wrong, it's not because the robot's behavior is inconsistent or unpredictable. It's simply because the detective doesn't understand it. Most satisfying of all, the ticking-clock ending neatly avoids the contrived feeling we've all gotten from less-successful stories. That clock is ticking because his partner, the robot, is who he is. His cooperation will end at midnight, for perfectly logical reasons, and our hero must set the world right before that happens.

That hero, Lije Bailey, is a classic mystery protagonist — a good cop, a family man, but a loner at heart. Solving this crime isn't just a job to him, because he values justice. He's a successful character, but we've met others like him. Before this book was published in 1954, nobody had ever met anyone like his partner, R. Daneel Olivaw, a machine who looks like a human being and whose newly programmed appetite for justice makes him act an awful lot like one. Dr. Asimov said that Daneel may be his most popular character. I know he's my favorite.

Asimov was one of us, a lifelong mystery reader. Actually, he was a lifelong omnivorous reader. His descriptions of the magical library of his youth take me back to the bookmobile that I ransacked weekly as a child. I remember exactly where my favorite books were shelved — Nancy Drew's adventures, Alfred Hitchcock's anthologies, and the long row of Robert Heinlein's juvenile novels. (Imagine my chagrin when I learned that Mr. Heinlein referred to his juveniles as "boys' books." Trust me, I was never a boy.)

When I hear the word "library," I feel an air conditioner blast out air with that peculiar bookmobile smell. (I think it was the ink for the machine that stamped the due date in each book.) When I see my own books in libraries, the book-loving child in me gets a shivery thrill.

Like Asimov, my path took me from the library to a science education. Also like him, I eventually left the science I loved for the literature I love even more. My mysteries don't incorporate science fiction (yet), but the science is there. A writer can't help putting herself into her work. Constructing my mysteries have required me to bone up on meteorology, geology, archaeology, physics…

And I love it.

Mary Anna Evans holds degrees in physics and engineering, and science crops up in her Faye Longchamp archaeological mysteries despite her best efforts to avoid it. *Relics*, the followup to series opener *Artifacts*, was published by Poisoned Pen Press in 2005. The next installment, *Effigies*, will be out in early 2007.

Terence Faherty on
The Estate of the Beckoning Lady aka The Beckoning Lady
by Margery Allingham (1955)

Margery Allingham's *The Estate of the Beckoning Lady* is the *Midsummer's Night Dream* of mystery novels, with an aged Puck, a "Fairy No-good," and lovers young and old who pair off or renew their vows. (Rereading the novel for this essay, I was pleased to rediscover these parallels to Shakespeare's comedy. I had just published *In a Teapot*, a novella that uses an attempt to film *The Tempest* as an excuse to transplant Shakespeare's characters and situations to the Hollywood of 1948.) Allingham was a Golden Age master and a writer's writer, adept at any kind of story she chose to tell. She most often chose the mystery, though she claimed the status of novel for her books and, in my opinion, made good that claim.

Her protagonist, Albert Campion, started life as a member of the silly-ass-detective school. He changed as the series progressed, growing more sober but somehow less solid, an interesting feat. Campion often works with clues as ethereal as himself. When a character complains of a message in flowers being "damned subtle stuff," Campion replies, "That's my line." This resonated for me when I first discovered Allingham. My amateur sleuth, Owen Keane, another self-effacing guy, once said, "The clues I sought were echoes and whispers that could hardly be heard." Campion would hear them.

Part of Campion's tendency to blend into the wallpaper was due to the mystery element in the books losing ground to whatever themes Allingham wanted to explore. In *The Beckoning Lady*, to use the shorter British title, the themes include love and marriage. Of love, Allingham, speaking through Amanda, Campion's beautiful wife, says: "Love isn't a cement. It's a solvent." A typically offbeat and insightful observation. One of the marriages considered in the novel, warts and all, is

Allingham's own. She and her husband, Pip, appear as Minnie and Tonker, two long-married sparring partners. They correspond to Shakespeare's Titania and Oberon, though they are fully drawn and very human characters. (All too human in the case of Pip/Tonker.)

There is a mystery, of course, and three unnatural deaths, a respectable total for a book whose action largely involves an elaborate garden party. And Campion does solve it, though he often seems preoccupied with the love lives of his friends. He is assisted by his manservant Lugg, the anti-Bunter, who was getting on when the series started and must be about 90 in this installment.

In addition to Lugg and Amanda, many other characters from earlier adventures appear in this late work, including at least one from the very first Campion book, *The Crime at Black Dudley*. I like occasional guest appearances in a long-running series; they reward a reader's fidelity. But all the cross-referencing could make *The Beckoning Lady* a bad place to begin exploring Allingham. I'd suggest *Death of a Ghost* for that.

For a writer, though, *The Beckoning Lady* can be a great study. For example, is the blizzard of exposition at the beginning of the book a weakness or a strength, underscoring as it does the confusion that surrounds the preparations for the party? And what of the flower symbolism used throughout? As already noted, Campion (who shares his name with a flower) receives a message in the form of a bouquet, each of whose flowers has a traditional meaning. (I lifted this idea, with appropriate acknowledgment, for my third book, *The Lost Keats*.) An aspiring writer can learn much from Allingham of character and setting and a more intangible element of fiction: atmosphere. Her specialty was what Agatha Christie recognized as "the fantastic and the real intermingled." As such she was the least earthbound of the Golden Agers and the one most encouraging to any writer who believes there are no limits to what the mystery can be.

Terence Faherty is the author of the Shamus-winning Scott Elliott private-eye series set in the golden age of Hollywood. He also writes the Edgar-nominated and Macavity-winning Owen Keane series, which follows the adventures of a failed seminarian turned amateur detective.

Ann Granger on
Scales of Justice by Ngaio Marsh (1955)

If there has been a writer who inspired me and set me on the authorial path it is Ngaio Marsh (1899-1984). The book I consider to be among her best is *Scales of Justice*.

Marsh's skill at setting the scene is rooted in her early training in the theatre. (She was a successful theatrical producer in her native New Zealand.) *Scales of Justice* opens with the district nurse, Nurse Kettle, cycling up a steep hill at the top of which she rests, panting, to look down on the hamlet of Swevenings laid out beneath her like a tapestry. She sees the countryside in the peace of a golden evening. Gazing at it, she decides it is perfect.

Poor Nurse Kettle is in for a shock! Beneath its calm, it harbours dark secrets, old resentments, petty spite and, in the case of one person, murderous resolve. This is a story of the sins of the fathers stretching down the generations to cast a shadow over the lives of their children. The cast of characters is beautifully and sensitively drawn. Lady Lacklander arrives on the scene described so: "the train of her old velvet dinner-dress followed her and the diamonds which every evening she absentmindedly struck about her enormous bosom burned and winked as it rose and fell." Eccentric Octavius Phinn is likewise described as wearing "a smoking-cap, tasselled, embroidered with beads, and falling to pieces."

Marsh writes not a word that is not there for a good reason. Both these pieces of description are symbolic. These two elderly people represent a once glittering world which is now long in the past and what's left is falling apart. They are a generation in the evening of their lives. Nor is Phinn's eccentricity just a quirk. His mind is suffered because he has suffered.

Nurse Kettle has arrived to sit with Sir Harold Lacklander, who is dying. Sir Harold knows he has little time and, whatever the cost to his own reputation, puts into the hand of a neighbor, Colonel Carterette, a document telling everything, with instructions to publish. In so doing, he unwittingly places in the honorable ex-soldier's hand a death warrant.

Marsh's detective is the intelligent and sophisticated Chief Inspector Roderick Alleyn. He is a quiet man who watches the scene and observes the players. He gathers scraps of information and weaves them patiently into the whole. When Alleyn comes to Swevenings one of his first encounters is with a cat. He stoops to pet it and a strong odour tells him it has been eating fish. Is this Marsh being whimsical? Not a bit of it. It is a vital clue. The reader mustn't miss it. Alleyn does not.

At the climax of the book, one of the characters tears Nurse Kettle's image of Swevenings to shreds in a speech that is a burst of vitriolic rage. It's a terrific piece of writing.

Marsh slices open human emotions and motives with the skill of a surgeon. Her eye is sharp but not unsympathetic. Her writing is always elegant, her plots ingenious, her characters human and real. Readers must stay on their toes. This is mystery fiction of the Golden Age at its very best.

Some time ago at a Malice Domestic convention then held in Bethesda, Maryland, I had the good fortune to meet Ngaio Marsh's cousin and was able to tell him of my debt to her and that she had, in truth, made me a writer. He replied, "She would have been very pleased to hear that." And it made me happy.

Ann Granger studied French and German at London University before working in British Embassies in various parts of Europe. She is the author of 21 mystery novels of which the best known in the United States is the Mitchell and Markby series of fifteen novels, the latest being *That Way Murder Lies* (St. Martin's, 2005).

Carl Brookins on
Strip for Murder by Richard S. Prather (1955)

A few years ago — make that decades — when I was a randy teen, I often browsed the city bookstores. One night I came across a new author. Richard S. Prather.

I don't remember the title of that pocket book. I just remember I was impressed — by the writing and the action. Later I went back to the same store on a hot summer night. There was another book by that same author. Its title: *Strip for Murder*. It contained one of the most hilarious scenes I have ever read in crime fiction. In the novel, Scott is hired to protect a woman who is seriously into the naturist movement in California.

This was a time when fiction's manly men took on the establishment, rode their lonely way through mean streets and either bedded or shot lovely women while righting wrongs; when the heroes of Guadalcanal returned from winning a war and a new group of uniformed young men headed to Korea. It was the time of a six-foot-plus, white-haired, former gyrene named Shell Scott. Weighing over two hundred pounds, Scott did not walk unnoticed into a crowded room, sporting a tweed jacket when the other men were in tails or tuxes. He had a jaundiced outlook, an eye for the ladies and a finely developed sense of right and wrong. His best male friend in all of Los

Angeles County was a homicide cop. The Shell Scott books reflect Prather's era, and the kind of crime fiction then being written, but Prather was somehow slightly out of tune, even when his muscular prose resembled that of his contemporaries.

"She was maybe five-six, with hair like copper and brass melted together by the sun, and had great big beautiful blue eyes... She breathed and I nearly fainted."

Strip for Murder is a judicious blend of direct, punchy action and Scott's "take" on local and world events. His observations, cynical, pithy and often amusing, place the novel in its time. The satire in the 34-book Shell Scott series is unmistakable and all encompassing, especially toward the genre in which Prather worked. Prather's pace, his sense of timing and his descriptive language are excellent. While sensibilities and attitudes, particularly toward women, may have changed over the intervening years, *Strip For Murder* is still a novel that holds interest. Here, Scott joins his client at the nudist camp: "Migawd, there were hundreds of them, capering joyfully around on the green. I'd been hired to find a killer in a nudist colony, and I was going to look pretty damned silly wearing nothing but my gun!"

My favorite scene occurs toward the end of the novel. Scott, undercover, leads members of the nudist colony in athletic events, when a sniper attacks. Scott's escape, since he can't shoot back, is a nearby hot-air balloon. Unable to reach the basket, he clings, exposed, to the dangling ladder and rises out of range to discover the balloon is being carried by the wind directly over the downtown business center of Los Angeles. It is noon on a work day and the city streets are thronged. Scott's naked and embarrassing plight is soon discovered by the crowds below. He is only saved when his ride is blown into an open window of the LA municipal building.

Shell Scott is conservative, modest, incorruptible and serious about his work. And like all good literature, *Strip for Murder* can be read as a cautionary tale of any time. When Sean NMI

Sean walked into my life and told me that Shell Scott was his hero, I knew right away I'd found a boon companion.

Writing has been part of **Carl Brookins'** life for almost forever. Television scripts, reports and articles. Now mysteries. *Inner Passages*, followed by *A Superior Mystery* and *Old Silver*, from Top Publications. His first PI novel, *The Case of the Greedy Lawyers*, from Five Star, is also in release.

Marcia Talley on
The Door Into Summer by Robert Heinlein (1957)

As the daughter of a career military officer, I hopscotched around the world, never settling anywhere longer than two or three years. At each new duty station libraries were my salvation, but most were on military bases, designed for young men between the ages of 18 and 26, and overstocked (in my opinion!) with westerns and science fiction. I never touched the stuff myself, and it rarely took me more than a couple of months to work my way along the mystery shelves through Margery Allingham, Agatha Christie, F.W. Dixon, Carolyn Keene, Ngaio Marsh, Dorothy L. Sayers and Josephine Tey all the way down to Phyllis Whitney before I ran out of books to read.

In 1958 my family was stationed in Taipei, Taiwan, and as I moped in the sadly deficient mystery section, the librarian — a handsome young Navy Lieutenant — escorted me to the science fiction section and asked me if I'd ever read Heinlein. I hadn't. "Try this one," he said, handing me a copy of a book called *The Door into Summer*. "I think you'll like it."

I didn't like it, I loved it! *Door into Summer* remains one of the few mysteries — along with Tey's stunning *Daughter of Time* — that is read and reread, packed up last and unpacked first, and whenever a copy is lost due to injudicious lending, the first to be replaced.

The year is 1970 and Dan, an inventor of ingenious labor-saving robotic devices, has been cheated out of his business by a crooked partner in cahoots with his traitorous, soon-to-be ex-fiancée. To escape his personal and financial woes, Dan opts for cryogenic suspended animation, but he won't go without his best friend, Petronius the Arbiter, "Pete," his ginger ale-drinking tomcat. Alas, Dan makes the mistake of confronting his double-crossing partners one last time. He gets the Long Sleep all right, but he wakes up dazed and blinking in the year 2000 without any money and without Pete. Following a trail of subtle clues, Dan unravels the past, travels back in time, and takes revenge on those who wronged him.

Heinlein wrote this book in 1956, and in it he predicted ATMs, computer-aided design, Velcro, Roombas and even the drug Ecstasy.

Science fiction? To be sure. Heinlein explains the theory of time travel so well that even I as a young teen teenager could understand it. Romance? You bet. In one of the most satisfying plot twists of all time, Dan gets the girl in an ending that has me groping for the Kleenex every time. But *Door Into Summer* is pure mystery, too. What else, with a cat — another staple of the traditional mystery — as a major character?

In fact, Pete may be my favorite feline in fiction. In the dead of winter he meows at every door, hoping that behind one of them it will be summertime. It's a metaphor for hope, and like Dan and survivors everywhere, I'm always looking beyond the darkness for that door into summer, too.

Marcia Talley is the Agatha and Anthony Award-winning author of *This Enemy Town*. Previous titles in the Hannah Ives mystery series include *Sing It To Her Bones*, *Unbreathed Memories Occasion of Revenge* and *In Death's Shadow*. She is author/editor of two star-studded collaborative serial novels,

Naked Came the Phoenix and *I'd Kill For That*. Her prize-winning short stories appear in numerous collections.

Roberta Isleib on
The Pink Motel by Carol Ryrie Brink (1959)

My family adored everything about our close-knit neighborhood in the New Jersey suburbs. It featured new split-level houses, block parties, gangs of children on bikes, progressive dinners for grown-ups, and just a short walk to school for kids.

Then my father was abruptly transferred to a job in Detroit, Michigan. My parents made the best of things, selecting a building lot in a brand new suburban development. Homeowners could choose from four colors of aluminum siding — white, yellow, tan and Georgetown green. My mother picked yellow: we were about to be wrenched from a yellow house that was our home. Maybe this color congruence would soften the blow.

Months later, we trailed our moving van into that Michigan neighborhood where we discovered rows and rows of pure white houses. Two out of a hundred or so were tan and only one was yellow — ours. My mother wept for the home she'd lost and for the embarrassment of our brassy yellow siding. It was way too late and far too expensive to change our minds.

Lonely and out of sorts, I buried myself in reading, including Carol Ryrie Brink's *The Pink Motel*. In Brink's novel, a middle-class midwestern family inherits a motel from a distant uncle. The parents and their two children travel to Florida over Christmas vacation to put the place in order and prepare to sell. They are astonished and somewhat horrified by the gorgeous, garish setting — coconut palm trees, a dazzling blue sea, and the pink, pink, pink motel.

"As soon as we can afford it," Mr. Mellon says, "we must paint the motel white or brown or gray, so that it will appeal to ordinary people."

While they clean up and make repairs, extraordinary guests trickle in — a magician, a painter with a hamper full of delicious treats, a lady with three clever poodles, a family intent only on their suntan, a woodcarver and two men who resemble gangsters. Uncle Hiram's old friends and guests and a local boy named Big show the Mellon children the mysteries of the motel and Uncle Hiram's secrets for living. As the story unfolds, a dognapping is foiled and so is the conventional, constricted mindset of the adult world.

Pre-adolescent children dominate the action in this novel. They are curious, open-minded and observant, and they take charge — even of the adults. As a shy kid in a new town, I imagined myself in the thick of the Mellon family adventures. I was there as the kids uncovered the magic of Uncle Hiram's pink legacy and helped their timid parents see the motel's charm.

"I wonder," Mr. Mellon muses in the end, "if we could always run the Pink Motel along the same lines as Hiram did?"

"Yes, yes," says Mrs. Mellon eagerly, "to keep it pink, to try to understand each other, to be happy here and try to make everyone else happy — that would really be nice!"

I had Brink's lovely story in mind when I began to write my own mysteries just ten years ago. Like the Mellon children, my characters, neurotic golfer Cassie Burdette and newcomer psychologist Rebecca Butterman, are amateur detectives and outsiders, too. I remind them that a lonely reader might be counting on them one day. We try to do what Brink did in the Pink Motel: care about our friends, question conventionality, keep an eye on the bad guys and stay open to magic.

Agatha and Anthony-nominated clinical psychologist **Roberta Isleib** took up writing golf mysteries to justify time spent on the links. After five Cassie Burdette novels, including *Fairway to*

Heaven and *Final Fore*, the first in her new series featuring psychologist and advice columnist Rebecca Butterman will be published in April 2007.

Philip R. Craig on
Watcher in the Shadows by Geoffrey Household (1960)

One writer who had a significant influence on me was Geoffrey Household. Household is best known for his famous thriller *Rogue Male*, but one of his other novels interested and influenced me more: *Watcher in the Shadows*. One of my early novels, *Cliff Hanger* (republished as *Vineyard Fear*) is, in fact, a bow to Household's *Watcher*. It, too, concerns a narrator who is being hunted by someone he doesn't know for reasons that he also doesn't know.

Household's novels are often written in the first person, a point of view that is excellent for mysteries, insofar as it enables the writer to withhold information from the reader, but that doesn't lend itself easily to the creation of suspense regarding the narrator's survival, since he or she has at least stayed alive long enough to tell the tale. It was Household's skillful use of the first person point of view to achieve tension in *Watcher*, a book that combines mystery and suspense, that influenced some of my own thoughts about writing and my efforts to achieve some of the effects he achieved.

I'll not try here to write a treatise on point of view. (Percy Lubbock said about everything concerning that subject in *The Craft of Fiction*.) Rather, I'll simply point out that a first person narrator can never know the thoughts or feelings of anyone else or know what's going on beyond his own hearing and sight. This ignorance of the villain's motives and actions makes for good mysteries, but makes it difficult to create the kind of tension that can be established through the multiple points of view that are typical of thrillers, whereby the reader first watches the hero, then the villain, etc., and, by knowing more than either character knows, experiences suspense about the outcome of their inevitable encounter.

Household, in misleadingly dry, simple language, manages to achieve both mystery and great tension in *Watcher* by leaving the doom of his first person narrator in doubt up to the last chapter. The narrator, Charles Dennim, is a very private man, living a quiet, small time scientific life in post-war Britain. One day a postman, trying to stuff a thick envelope through the mail slot of Dennim's door, is killed when the envelope explodes. Dennim was the obvious target, but why? The motive for the attempted assassination must lie in the past, so Dennim looks that way and determines that some act of his in World War II, when he was a secret agent in Europe, has led to this attempt at revenge. To defend himself, Dennim abandons his civilized life and goes to ground in rural England. The assassin is soon on his track, and as the killer closes in, Dennim learns who his enemy is and that he holds Dennim responsible for the wartime death of his wife.

Household establishes tension by slowly revealing that his narrator, Dennim, who is a scrupulously honest man, is not just a simple, gentle, scientist, but a man whose secret activities during the war were sufficiently ambiguous to have been both a benefit to his cause and a danger to others on his side of the conflict. Dennim is able to identify the man hunting him and to accept his motive as an understandable one, even while barely escaping sustained attacks on his life.

This is tricky stuff, and when I tried to write my homage to Household, I was confronted by the same difficulties he mastered in *Watcher*: how could my narrator find out who was hunting him and why? How could he defend himself? What should he do about the problem, if he managed to avoid being killed? How should he think about the assassin? Wherein did justice lie?

My novel *Cliff Hanger* was my effort to deal with these questions, and you can read it and decide whether I was successful. My recommendation is that you read *Watcher in the Shadows* and see how a master has done his work.

Philip R. Craig has written or co-written nineteen novels, sixteen of which are Martha's Vineyard mysteries featuring J.W. Jackson, a retired policeman turned fisherman. He received his MFA from the Iowa Writers Workshop and has retired as Professor Emeritus in English at Wheelock College. He and his wife live on Martha's Vineyard whence they enjoy traveling to sites of ancient civilizations.

JoAnna Carl on
Death and the Joyful Woman by Ellis Peters (1961)

Ellis Peters' *Death and the Joyful Woman* was the book that showed me the mystery could be a novel of character, as well as a puzzle and an adventure.

Of course, Peters wasn't the first mystery writer to create multifaceted characters. She happened to be the one who captured my imagination with that knack. And I know I'll never match her skill in creating characters who are fully human and who interact with realism.

Ellis Peters today is mainly remembered as the creator of Brother Cadfael. Many readers may be unfamiliar with her earlier books about George Felse, a detective in a small English city, his wife Bunty, and their son Dominic.

Death and the Joyful Woman won the Edgar Award for Best Novel in 1963. The book focuses on Dominic, and it is Peters' loving creation of an idealistic, exasperating and believable adolescent that makes me so fond of this book. The puzzle plot is good; the clues lead logically to the solution of the crime. The background about the history of an ancient pub sign is interesting. The action moves along briskly. Peters deftly describes a father-son relationship which includes friendship, respect, anger — even rivalry for a beautiful woman. But it's Dominic and his first venture into love that make the book a classic to me.

The plot can be summed up briefly. Dominic, who has just turned sixteen, falls for a local heiress, Kitty Norris, a beautiful, kind, and vulnerable young woman in her twenties. When Kitty is caught up in the killing of a ruthless tycoon, Dominic tries to keep her from becoming a suspect, and this effort forces him to betray his father. But his misguided attempt does not help Kitty; he finds instead that he has put her in greater danger. When Kitty is arrested, Dominic vows to prove her innocence, and he risks his life to save the woman he loves.

Notice that I don't say that Dominic's feelings for Kitty are a crush. Of course they are; when a sixteen-year-old boy falls for a young woman in her twenties, it's a crush. But Peters never fails to respect Dominic's feelings. Dominic loves Kitty with his whole teenaged heart, and Peters gives this love the dignity it deserves.

All of the characters receive this respect. For example, Leslie, the son of the slain man, bitterly disappoints his wife, not because he's mean or wicked, but out of concern for her and their unborn child. But when Leslie makes the right decision — the ethical choice — his wife's delight in his action is heart-warming and full of symbolism. All the characters, even the bad ones, are treated with this understanding.

Peters apparently hated to have bad, rotten people in her books. She told tales of people who do wrong because of weakness or doubt or ignorance or selfishness or anger or mistaken ideas of what would be good for other people.

Her books are gentle, but never unrealistic. Or at least they reflect the realities my life. I'm continually finding I've done the wrong thing because of weakness or doubt or ignorance or selfishness or anger or mistaken ideas of what would be good for other people.

Peters always saw right into the human heart, and she never saw more clearly than in *Death and the Joyful Woman.*

JoAnna Carl writes the Chocoholic mysteries, books featuring a young woman who is business manager for a company making luxury chocolates in an upscale Lake Michigan resort. Her latest book is *The Chocolate Mouse Mystery*. As **Eve K. Sandstrom**, she wrote two series laid on the southern Plains.

Eileen Dreyer on
The Ivy Tree by Mary Stewart (1961)

There are other books and other authors I could cite who affected my writing career. Nancy Drew got it started. When I was ten I ran through all of the Nancy Drews that were available and simply began to write my own. Dick Francis taught me the elegance of a well-laid clue. Elizabeth George, among others, honed my taste for the delicious feast that is the psychological thriller. But I have to admit that looking back on my reading and writing life, it was Mary Stewart who set me on the path I took.

Genre readers and writers, I believe, travel a specific course through their formative years toward their preferred area of fiction. My friends in romance tended to travel the Georgette Heyer/Dorothy Dunnett/Rosemary Rodgers path. My friends in mystery gravitated more towards Nero Wolfe and Agatha Christie. But there are those of us caught in between, who straddle both worlds, perfectly comfortable with not only the emotional depth of a good romance but the clean, taut lines of a mystery or thriller. I'm definitely in that camp. Given a choice, I'd take Hitchcock's *Notorious* over his *Psycho* any day.

I've often wondered why I ended up in that place. I happily acknowledge the formative influence of authors from Helen MacInnes to Alistair MacLean to P.D. James. But I believe my course was set the moment I picked up my first Mary Stewart.

Nancy Drew taught me at nine that girls could be tough and smart and cool. She instilled my love of suspense (after all, Nance was always getting into danger, usually in that cool red roadster). She laid out plot and rising tension and the concept of red herring. (Okay, I was only ten. But it wasn't tough to miss.) Trixie Belden taught me a sleuth could be married and still solve crime, and Cherry Ames taught me independence.

But when I was twelve, I graduated to Mary Stewart. I can't begin to describe the thrill of discovery. Here was an author who not only wrote intrepid heroines, but complex ones. She didn't just set a great stage (to a girl from the Midwest, there were no more exotic locales), but populated it with multifaceted characters. In a single book I went from a two-dimensional world to a three-dimensional one.

I learned that crime was as complex as people, and that it affected its victims in less than obvious ways. I learned that motives didn't have to be obvious, nor did justice. I learned that a hero could help a heroine solve her dilemma without doing it for her. I learned that danger not only spiced life, but relationships. For a twelve-year old, it was revolutionary.

But why *Ivy Tree* in particular? It was with *The Ivy Tree* that Mary took me a step further, a step that I echo in many of my own works. Mary Grey, the heroine, impersonates a missing heiress for money, not the most heroic of purposes. It is, of course, Mary Stewart's homage to Josephine Tey's classic *Brat Farrar*. But I didn't know that at twelve. All I knew was that Mary Grey was a character who wasn't immediately likeable or sympathetic to a girl raised on *The Lives of the Saints*. She wasn't heroic in the way I'd been taught to recognize heroes.

She was human. She was so human that I found myself rooting even harder for her by the end of the book. It was Mary Grey's very faults that endeared me to her.

To this day, nothing compels me more about a character than his or her human frailty. I consider true heroism to be the ability to endure in spite of it, and I love nothing more than the chance to examine it. Mary Grey is the first character I can remember who sparked that feeling. Mary Stewart is the first author I read who spoke to the intricacies of human character and the mysteries of true heroism. And, oh, yes, she always included a romance. A twelve-year-old couldn't ask for anything more. A nascent author couldn't ask for a better tutor.

Still straddling that fence, **Eileen Dreyer** (www.eileen-dreyer.com) writes suspense and short stories as herself, and romance as Kathleen Korbel. Her latest suspense is *Sinners and Saints* from St. Martin's.

Kit Ehrman on
Dead Cert by Dick Francis (1962)

If someone told you that a mystery novel written by a person you've never met would influence the jobs you take, the places you live, the way you spend your free time, even the people you meet, you would suspect that this outlandish tale had all the makings of, well ... mystery fiction. But believe me; it can happen. I've never had the honor of meeting Dick Francis, but his writing has influenced me in astounding ways, both personally and professionally.

My introduction to Francis' work occurred in 1978 when I discovered *Dead Cert*. First published in 1962, *Dead Cert* was Dick Francis' first attempt at fiction after writing for the London Sunday Express for sixteen years. Francis is known for writing compelling openings, and *Dead Cert* is no exception. The story opens in the middle of a steeplechase race in which the hero, Alan York, is resigned to finishing second as he watches his good friend, Major Bill Davidson, precede him over the second to last fence astride Admiral, the best hunter-chaser in the kingdom. Only this time, the unthinkable happens. Before the field can turn for home, Bill Davidson will be dead, and Alan York will be thrust into an irrevocable course of action that will nearly cost him his life.

Dead Cert literally takes off at a gallop, and the reader has little time to catch his breath as Francis excels at plot and ratcheting up the tension. York's casual statement that he intends to look into the "accidental" death quickly lands him in a well-executed trap at the wrong end of a knife. *Dead Cert* is brilliantly plotted, with each clue posing another more challenging question and propelling York into greater danger that culminates with a breathtaking cross country chase with York astride the big-hearted Admiral. Like all of Francis' heroes, York is capable, strong and intelligent, as well as honored and principled. Once he sets off to right a wrong, he's not likely to back down, but as he faces off with a cunning desperate villain, he realizes the outcome may very well hurt the woman he has come to love.

In true Francis fashion, *Dead Cert* is populated with varied and rich characters, and imbued with a strong sense of place. Francis' descriptions of the English countryside are wonderful, but it's in the jockeys' changing room and on the racetrack and in the stable yards, among the horses and grooms and jockeys, where Francis really excels. After reading *Dead Cert*, you'll have a good sense of the banter and camaraderie that takes place in the jocks' room. You'll know what it feels like to gallop a thousand-pound, high-strung thoroughbred at 40-miles-per-hour over a turf course with a five-foot-tall birch fence in your path.

Dead Cert provided me with such a strong insider's look into the world of horses and the magical bond that is possible between human and horse, I changed my career path. Simply put, I fell in love with the world Francis depicted, quit my government job, and embarked on a 25-year-long career working with and owning horses. When I turned to writing, his influence was there, as well. I owe him a great deal.

Dick Francis is the best-selling author of 38 mystery novels and the recipient of numerous awards, including three Edgars for Best Novel. He was named Grand Master by Mystery Writers of America in 1996 and is considered a consummate craftsman by his peers. It is no surprise that today's mystery authors cite this master of mystery, a classic artist if you will, as their inspiration. After all, before most of us ever put pen to paper, we were, first and foremost, fans of this wonderful genre.

Kit Ehrman (www.kitehrman.com) pens the Steve Cline mystery series. From the fancy show barns to the backside of a racetrack, the horses and settings are as integral to the stories as the mysteries themselves. Ehrman's latest, *Cold Burn*, unfolds on a breeding farm under threat of arson.

Monette Michaels on
The Moonspinners by Mary Stewart (1962)

In the summer of 1964, I picked up *The Moonspinner*s. From the opening line, Mary Stewart had this twelve-year-old girl hooked: "It was the egret, flying out of the lemon grove, that started it." Such a simple line filled with questions. Who is the narrator? Where was the narrator that she chanced to see an egret fly from a lemon grove? And what exactly had started?

From that little line, I traveled with Nikky Ferris, a young British woman, on a journey of discovery and danger. When

Nikky takes that first step off the beaten path to Agios Georgios, she doesn't know it yet, but she has changed her life forever. As she makes her way into the rugged mountains lining the Greek coastline, I tasted the dust Nikky's shoes cast into the air. I smelled the lemon flowers as she wends her way through the grove. I shivered at the coolness of the mountain water when Nikki pauses to rinse her hot, dusty hands. I shared her sense of isolation and the building anticipation that something was going to happen. When Lambos drops into her path, knife in hand, my heart jumped right along with Nikky's. What had started out to be a pleasant little getaway with her aunt in a sleepy little Greek seaside resort, has now become a life and death matter as Nikky's future becomes inextricably inter-twined with Mark and Colin Langley's lives — lives that had been changed forever when the brothers stumbled across mur-der in the wilds of Greece. And I was with her every step of the way.

What amazes me, now that I also write novels, is that the set up in *The Moonspinners* is done so effortlessly and in less than two chapters. There are no wasted words or lines in a Mary Stewart book. Just as the fabled Moonspinners spin the moon, Stewart spins her story, effortlessly and inexorably pulling in her reader.

So what is it about Mary Stewart's romantic suspense novels that has captured several generations of readers and influenced a generation of authors?

For me, other than the amazing settings and sense of place, it is her ability to create an atmosphere that holds you breath-lessly in its thrall from her novels' first words until the last. Her use of words rivals a poet's. No doubt about it: Mary Stewart is a master wordsmith. Added to her perfect selection of words is a superb sense of pacing. Each word, each line of text builds upon its predecessor, building tension and providing relief, only to escalate again until the final climactic scene. Her plots are a perfect balance of description, suspense and romance, and as seamless as a Mobius strip. This is why a whole generation has attempted to emulate Mary Stewart's style.

In my romantic suspense novels, I sweat every word, every line, striving to recreate the suspense-romance symmetry, the perfect pacing of a Mary Stewart novel. My villains are driven to commit evil. The heroes are strong; the heroines, just as strong or stronger. Fate throws them together, changing their lives for better — or worse, as the case may be. In my books, as in Stewart's, good always triumphs over evil, but sometimes the line between the two is a bit smudged. From lean first lines to the end, I strive to take my readers on just as breathless a ride as Mary Stewart always gave me. Do I do this as gracefully as she did? I only hope so. Time will tell.

A former trial attorney, **Monette Michaels** has written novels of romantic suspense, including *Fatal Vision*, *Death Benefits* and *Green Fire*. Her latest book is *The Case of the Virtuous Vampire* (LTD Books, 2005), which she describes as Perry Mason meets woo-woo. Monette and her pathologist husband divide their time between Carmel, Indiana, and Austin, Texas.

Michael Jecks on
The Night of the Generals by H.H. Kirst (1963)

It has to be the most difficult question to answer. How can a writer isolate which of so many books has been the greatest influence on his or her work?

In my case, I've been reading voraciously from an early age. Conan Doyle, Christie, Ellis Peters and hundreds of others have had their own impact at times. When I was younger, Tolkien gripped me; as I grew older, le Carré; more recently it's been George MacDonald Fraser and Michael Connelly. But one book that has always forced me to return to it was *The Night of the Generals.*

H.H. Kirst, a not very well known German writer, wrote this anti-war, anti-Nazi book set in two time periods: the razing of the Warsaw ghetto in 1942 and then Berlin in 1956.

It begins, naturally enough, with a murder. It's a sordid little death, a Polish prostitute is found stabbed, but her corpse has been savagely butchered after she had died. The murderer had slashed at her as though in an insane frenzy. Not enough to cause the hardened Engel any upset. At this stage in the war, all those involved in counterespionage in Poland have seen enough dead bodies. The German occupying forces have nothing to fear from a maniac who slaughters whores.

But soon the danger is spelled out. In the first few pages we meet Major Grau, Engel's superior, and Grau learns that a witness saw the killer leave the scene. And it was a German General.

And it's from this point (the ninth page in my well-thumbed book) that the story grips all the way through to the end. It's told expertly as a series of official reports, excerpts from conversations with witnesses, correspondence from that period, and diary entries, interspersed with simple narrative.

It should be a bleak, depressing tale. The story of a prostitute's murder, just one death in millions during the war, but Kirst makes Grau an inspiring investigator. He is kind, generous and humane, unlike so many of his comrades. The plot is entirely gripping, and is perhaps more of a why- rather than who- dunit. But I like that. In my own books, I tend to spend more time fleshing out the whys — the motives of the killers — than the simple novelistic trickery of concealing the identity of the murderer completely. I'm happier showing the reasons, the logic behind the death.

I do wish I could copy Kirst's style, though. By turns funny, serious, sardonic and biting, it has some very serious messages about man's responsibilities in wartime, responsibilities to the truth, to those who live under the soldiers' rule, to the individual troops. And at the end, there is the great responsibility: that of the investigator to expose the truth.

Especially when the criminal is a General who holds the fates of hundreds of thousands in his hands.

If you haven't read this book, please, go and buy it today. You won't be disappointed. It certainly had a huge impact on me, and I like to hope that my own work is as gripping in its own way.

Michael Jecks is the author of the Templar series. The books feature actual murders from medieval England. A past Chairman of the Crime Writers' Association, he's a member of the Society of Authors, Crime Writers of Canada, and founder member of Medieval Murderers. His latest book is *The Friar's Bloodfeud*

Sharon Short on
Harriet the Spy by Louise Fitzhugh (1964)

When I was eleven-years-old, I happened upon *Harriet The Spy* by Louise Fitzhugh.

At the time, I didn't know that the novel — published in 1964 — had already been out for eight years and was and is a classic of children's literature.

What I did know was that if I could meet Harriet, she and I would be (I hoped) fast friends.

Oh, we were different, but only in surface ways. She lived in New York City; I lived in Ohio. She had a nanny; I didn't know of anyone who had a nanny. But in many ways that mattered ... *we were just alike*. We both knew we would be writers when we grew up. We both kept notebooks and wrote what we REALLY thought.

So, during my sixth grade year, I read Harriet's story thirteen times. I kept track in my own notebooks.

I think I compulsively reread the novel because in many ways that mattered, we were also quite different. Harriet was far more daring — climbing into a dumbwaiter and sneaking down an alley to spy on grown-ups!

I was both shocked and inspired by Harriet's gutsiness. I realized that recording my own thoughts would not be enough to make me a real writer. I'd have to observe people. Take notes. Mull over what I'd witnessed. Come to my own conclusions.

So I started watching people more closely, recording snippets of conversation, observations. There weren't any dumbwaiters or alleys in suburbia, where I grew up. But... one could hide under windows behind ubiquitous suburban bushes (three green dots per house). Or, oh so casually and slowly, roller skate past the most interesting houses in the neighborhood. Hmm...

After sixth grade, I did not again read *Harriet the Spy* until recently. It was just as entrancing and scary and wonderful as I remembered it. However, upon this reread, I also realized something new... why Harriet nudged my subconscious self toward being a mystery writer.

As Harriet says: "Life is a great mystery." In all her spying and notetaking, the mystery Harriet is really trying to solve is: what motivates people? That tricky question, of course, is what the best mysteries attempt to answer.

And the answer to that question can be endlessly surprising. Harriet herself is surprised time and again by what she learns about the people she spies on. She thinks she knows what makes them tick, but then she observes something that surprises her. For example, when Mrs. Dei Santi discovers her grocery employee has been giving food away to hungry kids, she is so moved that she gives them even more. Writes Harriet: "That was a scene I'm glad I saw because I would have guessed that

Mama Dei Santi would have bopped him over the head…"

But Harriet also discovers the hard way that telling the raw truth can be dangerous. Harriet loses her notebook and her friends find it. They don't like reading her harsh observations of them and, in reaction, even shun her.

As Ole Golly, Harriet's beloved nanny, advises Harriet, sometimes you have to tell "little lies." She says, "Remember that writing is to put love in the world, not to use it against your friends. But to yourself you must always tell the truth." And so Harriet makes up with her friends… and converts her observations into stories she shares through the sixth grade newspaper.

I think that's just what mystery writers must do, espy human motivations and tell themselves the truth about those observations, and then convert those truths into the most deliciously entertaining "little lies" ever told: mystery stories.

Sharon Short (www.sharonshort.com) mixes humor with mystery in her Stain-Busting Mystery Series featuring stain expert Josie Toadfern. *Hung Out to Die* is the most recent title in the series; sample chapters are available at her web site. Short, who lives in Ohio, also writes a weekly humor column for the Dayton Daily News.

Dick Cady on
The Chill by Ross Macdonald (1964)

Like many youngsters growing up in the 1940s and possessed with an appetite for reading, I graduated from the Hardy Boys to Sherlock Holmes. By happenstance, I got an early taste for "adult" fiction, thanks to my older brother. He brought home paperbacks by, among others, John D. MacDonald, Mickey Spillane and Richard S. Prather. Thus at ages ten through twelve, I read books like *The Damned*, *Kiss Me, Deadly* and many of the Shell Scott mysteries. I was greatly influenced by movies, so it was an easy step, through my teen years, to read Hammett, Chandler and Cain. I was also much taken by *The Saint*, eventually read all of the Father Brown stories, and sampled widely of other mystery writers.

This happenstance followed me into high school. In my senior year, my English teacher fueled my interest in reading and writing, and did something that in later years probably would have cost him his job. He loaned me his copy of Henry Miller's then-banned novel, *Tropic of Cancer*.

While I thought I might want to write something myself, I felt drawn to what I considered Literature with a capital L. Joyce, Durrell, Mailer, Lawrence — these were novelists I admired, and for stage writing, Tennessee Williams. The first thing I wrote, in high school, was a short play filled with ersatz Williams. It was Bad with a capital B. Many years later, I dug the thing out and read it aloud to my wife, and we laughed hysterically. I shredded the manuscript.

In my twenties I decided to write a "spy novel." Instead of writing it, I over-wrote it. Another manuscript destined for the shredder. The journalism career by which I now earned a living imposed comfortable walls upon my ambition.

But if I did not write as much in fiction, I read voraciously, almost anything I could get my hands on, including plenty of mysteries. By and by, I encountered the extravagant praise bestowed upon Ross Macdonald by Eudora Welty and William Goldman. I became hooked. And in back-tracking on Macdonald (real name: Kenneth Millar), I read his award-winning 1964 mystery, *The Chill*.

If Raymond Chandler achieved something close to the perfect mystery novel with *The Big Sleep*, MacDonald achieved in *The Chill* the combination of ingenious plotting and powerful yet subtle prose which he brought close to perfection in his later body of work (*The Goodbye Look*, *The Underground Man*,

Sleeping Beauty, The Blue Hammer.) It's the kind of book one of my older mentors would call a "gasser," a word embodying the highest praise.

The Chill is a story constructed like a beautiful puzzle whose intricate twists and turns gradually and surprisingly blend to a single narrative pathway in which everything is smoothly and shockingly revealed in the final paragraphs. It brought to mind a Mickey Spillane quote I remembered from the paperback jacket of *The Damned* a half-century ago: "I wish I'd written this book."

When, years later, I wrote my first mystery, Ross Macdonald was one of the many ghosts of writers looking over my shoulder.

Luckily, I had the good sense to avoid attempting to imitate. Luckily, I had the sense to realize that inspiration, combined with hard work, might some day produce mystery fiction of some lasting merit. Time, as always, will tell.

Dick Cady is the author of *The Executioner's Mask* (2004) and the forthcoming *The Hangman's Noose*, both Sonny Ritter mysteries set in Indianapolis.

Gary D. Phillips on
Pop. 1280 by Jim Thompson (1964)

The version I read and still have of Jim Thompson's *Pop. 1280* is the 1984 Black Lizard reprint. The cover art depicts a portly lawman whose face is Glenn Fordish with a demonic simpleton's gleam. Three babes surround this guy — two blondes on either side of him, and a dark-haired beauty in the shadows hoisting a six-shooter.

The main character of the book is Nick Corey, the high sheriff of the Southern Potts County. He pretends to be just a lazy sort, at home with Li'l Abner and Daisy Mae. But in reality, Sheriff Corey is a womanizing, manipulating sociopath out to cut the best deal he can for himself.

Corey is in the family with Thompson's other demented murderous deputy, Lou Ford from *The Killer Inside Me*. Ford recognizes his sickness and is tormented about it; Corey just goes along doing these things and doesn't look back. It can be argued that Thompson used specific constructs over and over in his books — the deadly schizoid dames, the grifters, the conniving drunks, the small time graspers — but he knew how to mold that material and bring out the nuances of these scumbags to distinguish them one from the other.

The thing that always charged me about a Thompson novel was that you took the people as they were. Thompson wasn't much for wallowing in backstory or psychological underpinnings, his folks were just goldurn mean and nasty. They interpreted the world a certain way and proceeded forward in their own warped way.

Nick Corey is trying to fool readers as much as he's having it over the ones who think he's a dunce. Corey is contradictory, like a lot of Thompson's characters. While his peers are prejudiced against African Americans — the novel is set in the early 1900s — Corey exhibits a fairly broad view on race. Unlike other white men of his time who went to bed with black women, often using coercion or force, Corey comments that he's had "certain relations with colored gals" and to him, that reinforces their humanity. Though naturally in the Thompson mode, when he's arguing with a couple of good ol' boys about whether black people have souls, the conversation veers into discussion on bestiality.

There are several instances in the story where Corey tellingly lets the mask slip and the calculating mind maintaining the facade surfaces. There's a painfully comical scene where Corey is literally kicked in the ass by Ken Lacy, a sheriff a few counties down the river, and Buck, his deputy. Corey lands on his arm and Ken asks him sarcastically if he hurt it.

"I'm not positive," he says. "It could be either the radius or the ulna."

Corey recognizes that Buck notes this but then slips back into his slack-jawed yokel persona. Later, as if from the Karl Rove handbook of dirty tricks, he sets in motion a rumor that will blossom and defile his opponent Sam Gaddis for the position of sheriff, as the election is drawing near and Corey has to do something to keep his valued job.

Yes sir, Mr. Nick Corey does pretty much as he pleases. Unlike many a twisted Jim Thompson character, he gets away with his evil. There is no redemption, no comeuppance for the amoral man with a star of Potts County. It's not just that he performs his machinations to keep his job or to keep seeing the women he's messing with or working an angle to get some insurance money. As he says, "What I loved was myself, and I was willing to do anything."

Pop. 1280 is unapologetic. Corey has no journey of self-discovery. That is unless you count that in the end he says to a wary Buck, "I'm both don't you see? The fella that gets betrayed and the one that does the betrayin' all in one man!"

Read this sumabtich for the sheer joy and horror of the wicked ways of Sheriff Nick Corey.

Gary Phillips writes whatever he can get away with. His latest efforts are a graphic novel murder mystery set in post World War II Paris, and he has a short story in *Dublin Noir*.

Michael Allen Dymmoch on
Odds Against by Dick Francis (1965)

When I first read *Odds Against*, I didn't know a thriller from a cozy. I had no thought of ever writing a book myself. But decades later, when challenged to write an essay on a "classic mystery," I thought immediately of *Odds Against*. Why?

One reason is surely that the author has mastered the art of economic prose. His exposition is elegant in the sense used by scientists and mathematicians — there are no unnecessary adjectives or adverbs and only enough facts and esoteric detail to advance the plot and establish the bona fides of the protagonist. The index cards never show.

High stakes. Suspense. Reversals. Conflict. Danger. Francis employs all the classic elements of the thriller except the antagonist's point of view. He hooks the reader with the first sentence: "I was never particularly keen on my job before the day I got shot and nearly lost it, along with my life." Each sentence is crafted to follow its predecessor seamlessly and lead inevitably to the next. so that nothing confuses or stops the reader.

Humans seem to find facts easier to remember when they are related to one another and embedded in a story, particularly a familiar story. This may be one reason the same archetypal stories occur in all times and all cultures. Francis hangs *Odds Against* on the classic frame of the hero's journey popularized by mythologist Joseph Campbell: the hero lives in ordinary surroundings; he is called to action but is reluctant to heed the call; he is given aid by a wise older person or a mentor; he travels to the other world where he overcomes trials or challenges and may undergo a form of death; he returns to the world of the living with the grail or prize.

Permanently injured in a racing accident, championship jockey, Sid Halley, is drifting through life, "a pleasant cinder" of his former self, at a detective agency. He volunteers to trap a small time crook and is shot when he gets careless. While recuperating, Halley is challenged by his father-in-law to undertake a quest — to save Seabury Racecourse from unscrupulous developers. This "mentor" gives him a "gift" to help him accomplish the task, introducing him to his nemesis in a way that makes Halley seem an insignificant foe. Halley meets characters in his search for facts to stop the land-grab, people who help him, people he helps.

The hero's travel to the underworld is represented in the story's climax, which takes place beneath the stands of the racecourse. There Halley tests his wits, courage and strength against superior numbers, and brings back the grail in the form of permanent security for Seabury. Finally, he comes to grips with the loss of his former career. Dying in his life as a top jockey, he's reborn as a superior detective.

The symbolism in *Odds Against* is not obvious, but for those who notice, it adds an extra dimension — like finding the Easter eggs on your DVDs.

And *Odds Against* is also a damn good read!

Michael Allen Dymmoch is author of the Jack Caleb/John Thinnes mysteries, the latest installment being *White Tiger*. *The Fall*, a standalone romantic suspense, is out now along with an historical SF romantic suspense, *The Cymry Ring*. Michael is a Chicago resident.

Sam Hill on
Darker Than Amber by John D. MacDonald (1966)

It was 1973, I'd just come back from two years in Peace Corps in West Africa and moved to the Louisiana oilfields to build up a grubstake. I'd expected to end up on a drilling rig wearing cool overalls like Jim Hutton in *Hellfighters*, making a hundred dollars a day and beating off advances from women who looked like Katharine Ross. Instead, I ended up working for minimum wage on a roustabout crew, chipping paint off rusty pipes. On one trip out I borrowed a Travis McGee. The next trip, I bought the rest of the books in the series.

I picked *Darker than Amber* to talk about for the simple reason that I love great first lines, and Amber may have the second-best ever written: "We were about to give up and call it a night when someone dropped the girl off the bridge." The girl in question was Vannie, who'd just been fired from her job seducing middle-aged men into taking cruises where they were then robbed and murdered. She gets tossed off a bridge, wired to a concrete block, and is temporarily saved by Travis, only to be killed later trying to shake down her former colleagues.

At one level *Amber* is exactly what it sounds like: a hastily written period piece chock full of political incorrectness, clunky dialog, hastily sketched scenes and unlikely plot turns. But at another level, it is everything a novel should be: poetry exploring the murky middle ground where good and evil meet, and where not-quite-good people try with mixed success to save the not-quite-evil.

MacDonald was a wonderful wordslinger. I think it's *Amber* (but I'm not quite sure) where he describes a bedroom encounter as "belly slapping sex." In other books, he describes a town as "laying at the foot of the hills like a sleeping dog" and the airspace above O'Hare as "a ball of yellow lint." These lines work for MacDonald because his poetry is never forced or showing off. It is poetry to a purpose, language distilled to its purest state.

But we are readers of mysteries, and we do not read for poetry. We want storytelling, which MacDonald was wonderful at in a deceptively effortless, perfectly paced way. In *Amber*, there is a sequence in which Travis searches Vannie's former apartment, is caught and led at gunpoint to a beach where he kills his abductor and buries him in the sand. MacDonald owns us in those chapters, and the reader is not putting down the book and going to bed until he says it's okay.

And we want characters. MacDonald's real accomplishment was to create the modern villain. In MacDonald's world, criminals are not always likable and seldom admirable, but they are always recognizable. Vannie is a *slightly* worse version of us — selfish, a little lazy and prone to rationalization. And yet she does things that are *much* worse than any of us would ever do. In the end Vannie doesn't turn on her criminal colleagues because of a sudden fit of conscience or a realization that good, hard work is more rewarding. She turns because she realizes that sooner or later this gig has to end, and she wants to cash out. MacDonald's great insight is that evil and good occur at the margin, that in different circumstances Vannie might have been the local hairdresser. In different circumstances, some of us might have been Vannie.

I realize that I have used up my allotment of words and still not quite hit the center of the thing that makes me reread MacDonald every year or two and continually test my work against the standard he set. Maybe it goes back to where I started. What I'm trying to do is to create books that will last, that someone will discover and rush out to buy the all the rest of my work. And what creates lastingness is great storytelling, language and characters. That's what I think John D. did about as well as anyone ever has.

Sam Hill is author of three nonfiction books and two novels, *Buzz Monkey* and *Buzz Riff*. His work has been published in the Wall Street Journal, Fortune and Ellery Queen's Mystery Magazine. He spends his spare time advising CEOs and boards and speaking around the world. He and his family live in Chicago and Bloomington, Indiana.

Jeffrey Cohen on
Secret Agents Four by Donald J. Sobol (1967)

When I was nine years old, the most powerful role model I had was my father. That's what you're supposed to say, and in my case, it's true, but you don't want to read an essay about a man running a paint and wallpaper store in Newark, New Jersey. Still, to be honest, my father was the man I most looked up to.

But the man I really wished I could *be* was Napoleon Solo.

On *The Man From U.N.C.L.E.,* Robert Vaughn, as the aforementioned Mr. Solo, was about as cool a guy as there existed on the planet. He got to fly all over the world, banter with evil geniuses, shoot pretty much anybody he wanted to, kiss gorgeous women with mile-high hair, and he had a friend who was *Russian*, for goodness sake, even if he did speak with a British accent. How cool was *that*?

The problem was, Solo was an unattainable goal for a nine-year-old New Jerseyan. But Ken Mullins was not.

Ken, the hero of Donald (*Encyclopedia Brown*) Sobol's *Secret Agents Four,* proved that you could do all the things Napoleon Solo could do, even if you were a suburban preteen (minus the kissing, which was a little too yucky to consider at nine).

Okay, so Ken didn't have a Russian sidekick, but he had a dad who worked as a spy, and three friends (one of whom was an inventor!) who would listen to his theories about terrorists and spy organizations and take him seriously.

And this *wasn't* one of those lame stories where it all turns out that the kid was just imagining things. Ken's suspicions about nefarious doings in his Florida hometown don't just turn out to be someone rehearsing for a play or a paranoid fantasy brought on by the traumatic divorce of his parents. In fact, Ken's family is quite intact, and his father, upon hearing Ken's thoughts, acts on them.

The danger is real, and the characters have true emotions. When Ken believes he has shot and killed someone — even though it's one of the bad guys — he is seriously troubled by his actions. The reader is expected to empathize. This isn't just Cowboys and Native Americans in the backyard.

Maybe reading *Secret Agents Four* in my formative years didn't directly inspire me to write mystery novels, as it was another 33 years before I started *For Whom the Minivan Rolls*, my first book. But Sobol's talent for character and plot stayed with me, and his belief that humor can be incorporated with serious business certainly offered a lesson I've tried to learn. I also learned a little about the enduring power of the printed word.

I gave a copy of *Secret Agents Four* to my son, and then my daughter, when they were just about nine years old, and to them, it was brand new. But the sad fact is, in 1968 NBC cancelled *The Man From U.N.C.L.E.*

Jeffrey Cohen is the author of *As Dog Is My Witness* and two other Aaron Tucker mysteries, as well as nonfiction books *The Asperger Parent* and *Guns A' Blazing*. He still sort of wishes he were Napoleon Solo.

Judith Skillings on
The Photogenic Soprano aka Dolly and the Singing Bird by Dorothy Dunnett (1968)

"Men with bifocals: I spit."

With five short words Tina Rossi, narrator of Dorothy Dunnett's *The Photogenic Soprano*, takes center stage, establishes her personality and defines the conflict to follow. After more than 35 years, that opening sentence still glows like neon through the fog. A reminder that great stories, those that resonate and linger, grow from complex characters deftly revealed.

The Photogenic Soprano is a classic mystery. There are two central characters: Tina Rossi, and the object of her distaste, an enigmatic painter named Johnson Johnson. He discovers her with a dead body in her lover's apartment. Instead of handing her over to the police, he invites her aboard his yacht, Dolly, for a race through Scotland's Hebrides Islands. She agrees. It's the most expeditious way to search for her missing lover: an engineer who may be responsible both for the dead body and for scuttling a naval ship. Smiling, Johnson sets up his easel. He, too, is after the killer. Between squalls, he'll paint her portrait.

The mystery is intriguing. The tone is light; writing, urbane and witty. A British manor house mystery played out at sea. It has a restricted locale (the ports-of-call during the race) and a coterie of social sailors who know the gossip, but not enough about each other. There's a hint of military involvement, a bit of espionage, yards about rough sailing and a gloss of sophistication provided by the world of opera.

Yet, told by Tina Rossi, her voice lush with ego, *The Photogenic Soprano* emerges as much a character study as a mystery. Shedding Balenciaga frocks for foul weather gear, the singer is both dragged along and riding the crest of turbulent seas, some emotional, some real. She records them all. Or seems to. Her uncensored internal dialogue reveals her to be vain, opinionated, condescending, materialistic, capable, courageous and four pounds overweight. A candid portrait, suitable for framing. You have to adore her.

You do. Even if she finds Johnson, for whom the series is named, annoying. His banter cryptic. His appearance — "The black hair, the caterpillar eyebrows, the damn housefly bifocals" — irritatingly vague. He may be the painter but she wields her commentary like a palette knife, smearing one observation on top of the next to render Johnson Johnson as an impressionist original. Fully-fleshed and appealing, if seen from a few yards away. A master. Well, a man who is more than he seems.

As is the plot. And the skill with which the story unfolds. With masterful confidence the author lays out each strand of her seamless tale in plain sight, trusting Tina Rossi to dazzle the reader like sunlight on the sea and obscure the truth. The soprano is so believable she succeeds through countless rereadings. We take her words at face value because we know the face of, as she reminds us, "the only really photogenic coloratura soprano alive." We understand her character, her flaws, her prejudices. We sympathize. Even when the veneer is stripped away we don't feel cheated. She never deceived us; she made us not want to see.

On the last page, when Tina Rossi sets off downstairs to the nameless persons waiting below, she leaves behind a curious kind of optimism. The overwhelming desire to reopen the book and savor her tale again. To understand how she did it. Da capo. From the beginning.

"Men with bifocals: I spit."

Awed by Dunnett's novels, it took **Judith Skillings** three decades to try writing fiction. For her day job, she and her husband restore antique motorcars. Coincidently Rebecca Moore, the heroine of her series, does the same. Usually. In *Driven to Murder*, she's racing around Indy in vintage F1 cars.

Sandra Balzo on
Ammie, Come Home by Barbara Michaels (1968)

When I was asked the question, I didn't hesitate:
Ammie, Come Home by Barbara Michaels is the book that inspired me to become a writer.

What I didn't know, as I sat down to write this, was … why?

Ammie, Come Home is one of 29 novels written under the pseudonym "Barbara Michaels" by Mystery Writers of America Grandmaster Barbara Mertz. Mertz may be better known for her New York Times Bestsellers penned as "Elizabeth Peters," but it's the Michaels books I treasure.

Ammie, Come Home is what we mystery buffs call a "woo-woo." Woo-woo … like ghost — get it? I got it, and I loved it. So did a lot of other people. In fact, the book has been called the best American supernatural mystery of the twentieth century.

The story involves Ruth Bennett, owner of an elegant Georgetown home, and her niece Sara, who is staying with Ruth while attending college. One night Sara starts exhibiting behavior that can be explained as either possession or, well…insanity. The book, as reviewers have said, is "dripping with atmosphere," and downright "chilling." But under the chills and the atmosphere, *Ammie* is a story of the unlikely alliance — Ruth, Sara's scruffy boyfriend Bruce and college professor Pat MacDougal — that tries to save the girl.

I vividly remember reading it the very first time. I had checked the book out of the library and I devoured it the moment I got home. I can still hear the crackle of the plastic-covered book jacket as I opened it, feel the weight of the thick paper as I turned the pages, and suck in that lovely, musty "library book" smell as I read.

Since then, *Ammie, Come Home* has become comfort food to me. I return to it when I need to, just as I might to Campbell's Tomato Soup, or a McDonald's cheeseburger and orange drink, or — more likely these days — a nice cabernet sauvignon.

Like a glass of good red wine, *Ammie, Come Home* is comforting, but also complex. The art, the language: "... the terror began. It came slowly and slyly, like a trickle of dirty water through a crack." Or, in describing Sara, simply "the familiar, unrecognizable face."

I'm more aware of the nuances now, but when I first read *Ammie*, all I knew was that it took me to a place where good was rewarded and evil was punished — even after death. And despite the fact that most of the characters in the book weren't related to each other, and I was kin to none, I felt bereft when I closed the book. Like I'd lost a family.

I could regain that family, though, by simply opening the book again.

That was important to me.

You see, *Ammie, Come Home* came out in 1968. My father was dying of lung cancer. I was fourteen.

I was angry, because life seemed so unfair.

I was scared, because I knew my dad would die, as he did that December.

And I was ashamed, because my awful, secret fear was that my mother would die, too, and leave me alone.

In short, I was ripe for a fictional world to disappear into and, particularly, for a book like *Ammie, Come Home*. I needed to believe there was life after death. That family could form where there was none. And, most of all, I needed to believe that there was justice. Somewhere. Somehow.

And isn't that why we read — and write — mysteries after all?

To face our demons and triumph? To live our worst nightmares and still wake up in the morning?

Barbara Michaels helped me do that. Bless her for that.

Oh, and bless my mother, too. She's turning 90 this year.

Sandra Balzo's debut book, *Uncommon Grounds*, "puts a twenty-first century spin on the traditional cozy, replacing tea with coffee as the comfort beverage of choice," says Publishers Weekly. Balzo's first short story "The Grass is Always Greener" (EQMM) was nominated for an Anthony Award and won both the Robert L. Fish and Macavity Awards.

Mary Welk on
Murder to Go by Emma Lathen (1969)

I have a confession to make. Back in 1969, I, a married woman, fell in love with a total stranger. My heartthrob was an older man, a widower and respected New York banker who managed the daily exchange of millions of dollars on Wall Street. In his pinstriped suit and gleaming leather shoes, he was the exact opposite of my husband, a blue jeans and gym shoes kind of guy who visited a bank only on payday.

Two very different men, and yet I adored them both. Fortunately for all involved, only one of them was real.

Economist Mary Jane Latsis and lawyer Martha Henissart — aka Emma Lathen — created my fictional hero in 1961. Capitalizing on their knowledge of the financial world, they gave John Putnam Thatcher a job as senior vice-president of the third-largest bank on earth, the Sloan Guaranty Trust. They also made him a clever amateur sleuth.

Thatcher first appeared in *Banking on Death*, but I met him in *Murder To Go*. This tenth novel in the 24 book series tells the story of a $12 million loan made to Frank Hedstrom, the genius behind the Chicken Tonight restaurant franchise. Hedstrom plans to diversify his holdings with a take-over of Southeastern Insurance. Mayhem occurs when an outbreak of food poisoning puts the deal on hold. When the man responsible for sabotaging Chicken Tonight is murdered near Hedstrom's home, Frank quickly becomes the prime suspect.

As a reader, I admire Lathen's ability to craft believable yet tricky plots while infusing her stories with a modicum of humor. As a writer, I envy her competence in describing people. Instead of concentrating on her characters' physical attributes, Lathen relies on dialogue and personality traits to set them apart. She also leaves much to the reader's imagination.

Take, for instance, Thatcher's personal secretary. No Sloan

employee ever calls her anything but Miss Corsa, implying she's earned a respect that does not allow for familiarity. Lathen doesn't reveal her age. We suspect she's been with the Sloan for eternity, given that she vets Thatcher's visitors, decides which crises deserve his attention, and manages his schedule like a general manages a battle plan. She is the epitome of secretaries. When Thatcher says, "Miss Corsa, I have a few things that I want done immediately," Lathen writes, "Almost immediately they were done."

We suspect that this fine lady suffers the sleuthing of her boss with a raised eyebrow. Lathen tells us, "Miss Corsa greeted Thatcher's second return from Maryland with reserve. But when he arrived at his office the following morning without displaying any inclination for further travel, she thawed perceptibly. A second day of commendable attention to desk work, and Miss Corsa unbent enough to cater to weakness. 'I thought you might be interested,' she reported, handing him a newspaper with the relevant item carefully outlined in red."

Investment broker Tom Robichaux is described as "a man of far-flung interests" who claims "no woman really knows how to cook." Lathen says of him, "There had been Alphonses, Pierres and Etiennes in the Robichaux kitchens to match the Amandas, Glorias and Brendas in the drawing room." Not hard to visualize that character despite the lack of physical description.

Thatcher himself is even easier to imagine. "Thatcher lacked Tom Robichaux's capacity to harrumph his way through life's vexations. Nor did he resemble his eminent subordinate Everett Gabler, the personification of virtue confronting decay and degeneration. Thatcher was a man to take things as they came. He rarely wasted time or energy on what might have been."

The perfect banker. The perfect sleuth. And my kind of man.

Mary Welk has drawn on her experience as an ER nurse to

successfully knock off sixteen characters in four award-winning novels. Her latest mystery, *The Scarecrow Murders*, deals with the trials and tribulations of motherhood and proves once again that even intelligent women can sometimes produce foolish offspring.

Michael Z. Lewin on
The Goodbye Look by Ross Macdonald (1969)

I was already a married person when I began to read detective fiction. My then-wife introduced me to Raymond Chandler. She'd found him when a high school English teacher told her, "If you must read junk, then at least read good junk."

After I finished Chandler's novels, I discovered Ross Macdonald. By that time — the mid-'60s — Macdonald was being acclaimed as Chandler's rightful heir. Sententious literary critics even allowed as how he might just possibly be a serious writer despite his writing in a genre. While I admire a lot about Chandler, it took Macdonald's books — which made the family a legitimate central axis for mysteries — to make me want to try writing mysteries myself.

But although Macdonald's oeuvre prepared the ground, it was *The Goodbye Look* that actually got me going.

The Goodbye Look came out in 1969 and because I had a job and had just sold my first book — a nonfiction classic called *How to Beat College Tests* — I bought the new Macdonald in hardback. I read it quickly, slurping up some of the language delights along the way: "Pacific Street rose like a slope in purgatory from the poor lower town to a hilltop section of fine old homes." "The girl was wan with jealousy." "His eyes were black and glistening like asphalt squeezed from a crevice."

Chandler disliked Macdonald's early "pretentiousness in the phrasing and choice of words." Chandler suspected they were "compensation for a lack of some kind of natural animal emotion." But I always enjoyed the language in Macdonald and if sometimes it's a bit much I'll tolerate the excesses to get the goodies. We mustn't take ourselves too seriously, eh?

The Goodbye Look has a typically complicated story, along with Archer getting a bit of nookie and the kind of little plot touch I've always liked — characters who break into a house in order to put money into a safe. A good read.

But *The Goodbye Look* served another function for me. Like so many books of the genre, its plot was far too complicated for my poor brain to keep track of. I got the idea to go through the book again and make a chart of the story to see if it really did hold together and follow its own logic. So I went back, chapter by chapter, fact by fact, and tracked Macdonald's story.

I found no errors of fact or logic. That would not surprise me now, knowing as I do more mystery books and many more writers. But back then — summer of '69, when the Mets were still in last place — analyzing this Ross Macdonald classic was a task that fascinated me.

And one that stayed with me, even during the following months when the Mets won the Series, my first child was born, and we drove across the country to LA to show off little Liz to her grandmother.

It was in LA, in December, that I passed a little spare time by beginning to write a story with a private detective in it. The story was about a teenager who was trying to find her biological father and although Albert Samson was no Lew Archer, the story, which later became *Ask the Right Question*, certainly owed its existence to *The Goodbye Look*. But, where to set it…? I know. How about… Indianapolis…?

Most of **Michael Z. Lewin's** (www.MichaelZLewin.com) mystery novels are set in Indianapolis, where he grew up. The latest is *Eye Opener* (Five Star, 2004) which revisits his Indy private eye, Albert Samson after many years. For more information about Mike's books, stories, plays and other interests try his web site.

Rhys Bowen on
The Blessing Way by Tony Hillerman (1970)

I had grown up on those ladies of the Golden Age of mystery — Agatha Christie, Dorothy Sayers, Ngaio Marsh. I had read all their books, finding them light and entertaining and enjoying the whodunit aspect. But they never moved me; they never touched my soul. I never wept over the body in the library.

In the early 1970s, I found myself stuck at home with young babies, a life very different from the hectic pace of my previous career. I retained my sanity by frequent visits to the library. One day a book on the new mysteries shelf caught my eye. It was *The Blessing Way* by Tony Hillerman and it was quite different from any mystery I had ever read. From the first page where a tribesman, alone on a mesa, chanting prayers to various gods for the success of his hunt, encounters a Navajo wolf, my skin prickled and I felt as if I had been bewitched and transported into another world. Even his sleuth was completely different from the detectives in the books I had read — a young Navajo policeman, trying to straddle two cultures while bringing justice to both. I was an Englishwoman, newly arrived in California. I could appreciate that!

The pages were alive with Navajo culture, every part of it accompanied by appropriate chants. The landscape, the weather, fauna and flora of the Southwest were all so vivid that I felt I was there, walking on that red earth, watching the thunderstorms roll in across the mesa. I had never read a mystery before in which the milieu was as important to the story as the crime, or where the crimes sprang from the clash of cultures. It was like taking a mini-vacation to a strange and exotic place. I became an instant and devoted Hillerman fan.

As I read more of his books, I became fascinated with his insights into the Navajo mind. For example, I was blown away when I read that revenge could never be a motive in a Navajo killing because they had no concept of revenge. The insights were as exciting as the tightly written mysteries.

Later when I decided to write mysteries of my own, I knew exactly what kind of book I wanted to write. I wanted to be able to take my readers to another time and place, like Hillerman. For me the obvious place to write about was Wales. I had spent childhood summers with my mother's family in a Welsh village, where most inhabitants spoke Welsh as their primary language. I had hiked those mountains and been drenched in sudden storms. I wanted to share its different and unique culture and way of life with my readers. So I created a sleuth who arrives with his own set of demons and tries to find peace in a small Welsh village.

Writing about turn-of-the-century New York was a bigger stretch and bigger challenge for me, but it was a time that has always fascinated me, with one foot in the Victorian age and the other in the fast-paced modern world. So many people pouring in from all over the world, creating a melting pot of rich and different cultures — a society ripe for juicy and varied crimes! And so Molly Murphy became my Joe Leaphorn or Jim Chee, leading me through the back alleys of the Lower East Side as she in turn straddled cultures. With each book I write, I enjoy the mini-vacation of my own creation.

And I still look forward to each new Hillerman book. I have always been amazed and embarrassed when fans travel long distances to my signings or treat me like a celebrity. However, when I finally sat beside Tony Hillerman at a joint signing, I was completely tongue-tied and then babbled like an idiot. I guess we all have our own heroes.

Rhys Bowen has been nominated for every major mystery award, including the Edgar, and has won both the Agatha and Anthony. She writes two series, the Constable Evans mysteries set in North Wales, and the Molly Murphy Mysteries set in 1901 New York City. Her latest books are: *In Like Flynn* (Molly Murphy) and *Evan Blessed*.

Zoë Sharp on
The Day of the Jackal by Frederick Forsyth (1971)

I can still remember the first time I read Frederick Forsyth's seminal novel about a plot by the OAS to assassinate the French President, General Charles de Gaulle, in the early 1960s. It read like fact, not fiction, told in a straightforward but compelling documentary style. Up until that point my forays into crime fiction had been slightly more fanciful — the likes of Leslie Charteris' The Saint, or Dorothy L. Sayers' Lord Peter Wimsey. This pared-down matter-of-fact style was something exciting and — for me — very new.

Nevertheless, despite its effect on my youthful reading habits, I hesitated over choosing *The Day of the Jackal* in this case. Is it really a mystery or a thriller? In my 1974 edition, the plot is presented to suggest this is a fictionalized account of a factual event. It says:

In the spring of 1963, after the last conventional attempt to assassinate President de Gaulle had failed, Colonel Marc Rodin, Operations Chief of the OAS, launched the plan of the Jackal.

The Jackal was an anonymous Englishman who came literally within an inch of destroying de Gaulle and possibly changing the course of world history. Frederick Forsyth's brilliantly researched novel reveals how the assassin was recruited; how much he was paid; the intricate planning that went into the attempt; the international security net that was set up (but failed) to trap him; the fantastic chase across the Continent in which he kept only a step ahead of his pursuers; and the unprecedented security measures the French were compelled to adopt to save the President from the most ruthless assassin known to modern times.

The intended crime is known from the very outset, as is the fact that the mysterious hitman fails to complete his contract, and it's often said that the very definition of a thriller is to prevent something terrible happening, rather than solving who-dunit after it already has.

The forces of law and order, as represented by Commissaire Claude Lebel, do not really get to work until halfway through the book. Lebel is a quiet unassuming little man, hen-pecked by his domineering wife, but commanding the respect of his colleagues. An unlikely hero. By contrast, the Jackal is tall, blond, and good looking, a man who enjoys the finer things in life, and has no trouble either seducing a baroness or being picked up in a gay bar.

The plot reels you in and keeps you hooked as the Jackal's meticulous planning comes slowly unstuck in the face of Lebel's dogged police work. It is indeed brilliantly researched, with the method the Jackal uses to obtain a false passport still actually possible until only a few years ago. It is one of the few assassination books that actually has the hitman taking his newly fabricated custom rifle to a quiet spot to test it and zero the sights.

Having read the book again before I started this piece, I found it still an inspiring piece of work. In some ways I expected to be disappointed by it, to find that I'd grown more sophisticated in the intervening years and it no longer gripped me the way it once did.

And yes, there are areas where some editing could have improved the prose, where the odd section could have been tightened and refined to greater effect. But disappointed? No. Far from it. It's still a riveting story, superbly told, and I'd recommend it to any aspiring crime or thriller writer as a prime example of a rattling good read.

Zoë Sharp writes a series of crime thrillers featuring her ex-army-turned-bodyguard heroine, Charlie Fox. *First Drop*, published in the US by St.Martin's Minotaur in 2005, was shortlisted for Best British Crime Novel 2004. Zoë lives in the English Lake District, and is married, but would rather have a motorcycle than children.

Frankie Y. Bailey on
Murder in the Walls by Richard Martin Stern (1971)

When I reread *Murder In The Walls* for this essay, I was transported back to my initial encounter with the Johnny Ortiz series. Set in Santo Cristo, New Mexico, in this first book in the series, a city planner has proposed a road that would run through the historic house owned by Flora Hobbs. For years, Flora, a genteel widow from the East, has been using her house as a brothel, but the house dates back to the Spanish settlers. Anthropologist Dr. Cassandra Enright rallies support to save this piece of local history. Meanwhile, Lt. Johnny Ortiz investigates two homicides. One involves a bail-jumper who has been found dead on the mesa near Cassie's dig. The other victim is one of Flora's girls, found murdered in her room. After there have been two attempts on his own life, Johnny tracks the killer back to the mesa — highlighting one of the strengths of the series, Stern's use of his Southwestern setting.

When I first read this book, I knew little about New Mexico

and even less about mystery writers. Richard Martin Stern taught me a bit about both. Although I never had the opportunity to meet Stern, we did correspond on two occasions. The first time was when I was a teenager. I was browsing the mystery shelves in my public library when I stumbled across *Murder In the Walls*. I gobbled up the rest of the books in the series, and then I wrote a fan letter. I had never done anything like that before. I don't remember how the idea occurred to me. But I wanted to tell Stern how much I liked his series and what it meant to me. I wanted to tell him how terrific it was to discover Cassie Enright, a smart, competent professional, who was Black — at least on her mother's side — and who could hold her own with his detective. I liked too the fact that Johnny Ortiz was Apache-Spanish-Anglo. I thought all that "cultural diversity" — a phrase not yet in vogue — was really "cool." I was thrilled to find protagonists with whom I, a Black girl growing up in Danville, Virginia, could identify.

I wrote to Stern, and he wrote back to thank me for my letter. Years later, we corresponded again. With a brand new Ph.D. in criminal justice, I was working on a book about Black characters in detective fiction. I wrote Stern to ask if he would take part in a survey I wanted to include in the book in which I asked some authors questions about the portrayal of Black characters. Stern not only agreed to participate, but he also sent me the galleys of the new Johnny Ortiz book that he was about to publish.

I never met Stern, but I had the impression of a man who was gracious and kind, and who had a sense of humor. When I created my own mystery series, Richard Martin Stern's Johnny Ortiz series was in the back of my mind. As a Black female mystery writer, I come from a different perspective, but Stern provided me with my initial blueprint.

Once critically-acclaimed, Stern has been eclipsed by other Southwestern mystery writers such as Tony Hillerman. But *Murder In The Walls* remains a classic. I discovered the

Southwest — and cultural diversity in the mystery novel — with Johnny Ortiz and Cassie Enright. It was my pleasure to return to Santo Cristo.

Frankie Y. Bailey is the author of the Lizzie Stuart mystery series, including *Old Murders* (2003). She is author of Edgar-nominated *Out of the Woodpile: Black Characters in Crime and Detective Fiction* (1991) and co-editor with Steven Chermak of Anthony and Macavity-nominated *Famous American Crimes and Trials* (2004).

Sarah Stewart Taylor on
An Unsuitable Job for a Woman by P.D. James (1972)

A couple of years ago, I had the chance to ask P.D.James why she only wrote two mysteries featuring her young private detective Cordelia Gray. She explained that she'd been dismayed when the BBC production of the Cordelia Gray mysteries had taken the character in improbable directions. What had happened, James explained, was that Helen Baxendale, the actress who was playing Cordelia, had gotten pregnant during filming and so they had written the pregnancy into the adaptation, giving Cordelia an ex-lover with whom she was no longer in touch. James was so outraged at what she saw as a betrayal of Cordelia's nature that she decided to give her up entirely.

There was real indignation in her words, and I remember being impressed by James' certainty about just what Cordelia would and wouldn't have done, just as I'd been impressed by what a precisely drawn and compelling female sleuth she had created when I first discovered Cordelia Gray six years ago.

I was working on a directionless and hopeless literary novel when I read *An Unsuitable Job for a Woman* for the first time, and the novel absolutely wowed me. I loved its precisely crafted plot, its academic setting, its shocking solution and long denouement. Above all, the novel showed me what was possible within the so-called limits of a genre novel.

I had been leaning toward the form for a couple of years, writing plotless short stories and parts of novels that always seemed to have dead bodies in them. But when I found Cordelia, I decided to try to write a mystery. My own series character, Sweeney St. George, a young art historian with an interest in death and gravestones, had been knocking around in my head for years, but as I fleshed her out, I was inspired by James' alternative to the sassy, gun-toting, hard-as-nails female literary detectives who had never quite rung true for me. She showed me that I could make Sweeney the kind of character I had always wanted to write about: a complicated, damaged, introspective young woman with an abiding curiosity about life and death and why human beings do the things they do.

I think *An Unsuitable Job for a Woman* is a terrific little novel. By little I mean that there's a simplicity about it that makes it feel beautifully compact. James doesn't burden Cordelia with subplots or personal entanglements. She merely gives her a question to answer, and our sleuth sets about answering it in her methodical way. The question, posed by an eminent Cambridge scientist, is why his son quit university and killed himself, for no reason that anyone can imagine.

Cordelia possesses an evolving sense of justice about the whole thing. At first, she feels she must discover why Mark Callender killed himself because she has been hired to do so. But as the water gets muddied, she feels she must discover the truth because she has come to care for Mark.

I have now read *An Unsuitable Job for a Woman* many times and it never fails to reveal something new. James doesn't shy away from literary conventions, threading ambitious moments of symbolism through the plot. There's our heroine's dramatic escape from a well, which James fashions as a kind of rebirth for Cordelia, whose own birth brought about the death of her mother. And of course there's Cordelia's Shakespearean moniker and the way in which allusions to her namesake reverberate throughout the plot as James writes about loyal and disloyal children.

I confess that I sometimes daydream that despite her indignation, James has a store of unpublished Cordelia novels somewhere, in which Cordelia grows older, further develops her skills as a detective, perhaps even becomes romantically involved with James' other detective, Commander Adam Dalgliesh. (This must be the ultimate P.D. James fan fantasy.) I respect James' decision to give up what she saw as a literary creation tainted by the necessities of actors and screenwriters, but Cordelia is one of those characters who has become something like a friend to me, very real and very familiar beyond words on a page, a testament to her creator's skill and humanity.

Sarah Stewart Taylor (www.SarahStewartTaylor.com) writes the Sweeney St. George mystery series, featuring a young art historian who specializes in gravestones and funerary art. 2003's *O' Artful Death* was nominated for an Agatha Award and 2005's *Judgment of the Grave* was a Booksense Notable Book. She lives in Vermont.

Jeremiah Healy on
The Godwulf Manuscript by Robert B. Parker (1973)

Okay, I admit it: I'm troubled that a book appearing when I was already 25-years-old could be considered a classic. But that's how this recovering lawyer views Robert B. Parker's *The Godwulf Manuscript*, the novel that introduced readers to Boston private investigator Spenser.

I've come to know Bob pretty well over the years, as he was

good enough to sit down in 1985 with a newbie crime writer over drinks in Boston to explain how publishing and Hollywood really worked. It's hard to believe that Bob himself was barely 30 when he wrote *Godwulf*. The hardcover edition appeared from the Houghton Mifflin Company in 1973. As a fan, though, I didn't "discover" *Godwulf* the book or Bob the author until I picked up a copy of the 1975 Berkley Medallion paperback in 1978, two days before my wedding. I'm not sure whether it says more about his writing or my sex drive, but I stayed up in a peacock (please, no puns) wicker chair the third night of my honeymoon until 2:00 AM in order to complete the novel in one sitting.

The storyline is easy enough to summarize, but, frankly, I'm not going to bother, because plotting isn't the reason I've chosen *Godwulf* as my classic. Instead, I'll rely on chapter one's opening line: "The office of the university president looked like the front parlor of a successful Victorian whorehouse."

I mean, come on. Who could not think that he or she had found a diamond? And I use "she" advisedly. One of *Godwulf's* many attributes is that the Spenser of the opening book is sexual without being sexist, and therefore appealed to female readers starved for a male hero who wouldn't have offended them on a real-life date. Beyond that, Bob "evolved" Spenser from a stud who beds (separately) both mother and daughter in the same family to a monogamous knight by the end of the next book, *God Save the Child*, which introduces Susan Silverman as the investigator's continuing love interest. This sea-change turned the stereotypical, sexually promiscuous male private investigator into someone of courage and honor both genders could applaud. Frankly, it also gave me the idea to have my fictional private investigator, John Francis Cuddy, be a widower who stays faithful to the memory of his dead wife, even to speaking with her over her gravestone.

Another reason why *Godwulf* should be considered a classic

is that it made a location other than New York City or Southern California a credible setting for a hardboiled private investigator novel. Perhaps Sue Grafton's Kinsey Milhone, residing in the same fictional Golden State town "Santa Teresa" as Ross Macdonald's Lew Archer, could have seemed credibly traditional by locale if not gender. But Jonathan Valin's Harry Stoner in Cincinnati, or my John Cuddy (also) in Boston or even Sara Paretsky's V. I. Warshawski in Chicago? I'm not so sure.

Finally, I think *Godwulf* is a classic in a Major League Baseball metaphor. The most collectible — and, therefore, valuable — sports card featuring an eventual Hall-of-Famer is that player's rookie one. Robert B. Parker is unquestionably such an enshrinee, and *The Godwulf Manuscript* constitutes his terrific first season.

Jeremiah Healy, a graduate of Rutgers College and Harvard Law School, is the creator of the John Francis Cuddy private investigator series and (under the pseudonym Terry Devane) the Mairead O'Clare legal thriller series, both set in Boston. He recently finished a term as the President of the International Association of Crime Writers.

John Lescroart on
The First Deadly Sin by Lawrence Sanders (1973)

While many of my contemporary writing colleagues were devouring their Chandlers and their Hammetts, I was majoring in The Continental Novel in Translation at UC Berkeley, reading Tolstoy, Dostoyevsky, Camus — the light stuff. It wasn't until I was out of college in 1970 that I stumbled upon my first Nero Wolfe novel, which of course led to the rest of Stout, then to Conan Doyle, Christie, Marsh, James and a dawning realization that these mystery authors were onto something good. While *Crime and Punishment* was an important work of literature, the translated Russian made for a slog of a read. By contrast, the mysteries I read just flew by, providing hours of pure enjoyment.

I was not reading simply to pass the time. As someone with authorial ambitions, I was wrestling with the question of the kind of book I eventually wanted to write. On the one hand, I hoped to explore serious personal and societal themes with fully-developed characters and a literary sensibility; on the other, it seemed important to have fun and to provide enjoyment — I didn't want to write books that no one would want to read. These two inclinations seemed contradictory.

Then, in 1973, Lawrence Sanders' novel *The First Deadly Sin* arrived in bookstores. I'm sure that one of reasons for this book's success — and certainly the reason I bought it — was its title. The deadly sins are the very meat of most of the great written works. Great literary themes are driven by conflicts arising from pride, greed, lust, envy, gluttony, anger and sloth. A book entitled *The First Deadly Sin* would seem to promise a profoundly serious intent.

It is immediately apparent that the book falls into the category of genre suspense fiction, and the subcategory of police procedural. Surely this couldn't qualify as "real" literature. Here was a vicious psychopath with the unlikely name of Daniel Blank. His pursuer, a retired policeman (with a dying wife) named Francis X. Delaney, could have been rendered as a cliché plucked from the pages of the pulps.

But as I read this book, I realized that the development of these indelible characters had become, in fact, the plot. Events and murders pile on each other. There is action and searing suspense, but these men are not in the book to propel a reader to a conclusion — their existence and orchestrated fandango is the very essence of the book.

Here I found, at last, the synthesis of a literary sensibility and the narrative drive of a thriller. And the development of true depth of character — ostensibly the exclusive domain of the literary novelist — was also the most effective plot-driving technique I had run across to date.

Further, within the gruesome context of a modern manhunt, this book dared to be truly funny and even internally irrelevant. It risked long passages that did not "further the plot" — all of Delaney's obsessive (and fantastic) sandwich-making, his paranoid lock-up routines for his house, or his visits to his wife's sickbed. Without all of these "non-essential" elements, it would have been a forgettable book.

The dichotomy that I'd once believed was absolute between literature and genre fiction was itself a fiction. One could develop serious themes in books that might reach a popular audience. And the characters in those books could be superficially ordinary — people we might know in our daily lives, such as Dismas and Frannie Hardy, or Abe Glitsky — whose literary credentials as perhaps emblematic human beings only become apparent in the crucible of crisis. Hence my decision to allow Hardy and Glitsky to be married and have families; likewise, Hardy's elephant collection, his dart playing, his black pan and all the cooking, drinking, and restaurant-going in my novels; the banter between friends and spouses.

Despite the refrain from some critics that the mystery/thriller genre must always fail to qualify as literature, or that a compelling plot is a bar to literary significance, *The First Deadly Sin* would suggest otherwise.

John Lescroart is the New York Times bestselling author, most recently, of *The Hunt Club*, as well as the thirteen novels of the Dismas Hardy/Abe Glitsky series. A multiple nominee for various mystery awards, his novel *Sunburn* was also the recipient of the 1978 Joseph Henry Jackson Award for best novel by a California author.

Dan Fesperman on
Tinker, Tailor, Soldier, Spy by John le Carré (1974)

Until the day I first made the acquaintance of Mr. George Smiley, the universe of the novel existed for me on two separate planets.

One was a sphere of great gravity, a place where every selection might also be found on an English major's syllabus. From the manly heft of Hemingway to the wacky jolt of Vonnegut, this was a destination not just for enjoyment but also for the challenge. On this planet, not only was there no easy ride, you sometimes had to get out and push.

There was also Planet Genre, realm of cheap thrills, fried foods, easy sex and other dreamy confections. You might spend a weekend of late nights with Travis McGee or James Bond. There was plenty of action, and you could always count on the good guys. Cerebral hedonism without the hangover.

Then, on the recommendation of a friend, I cracked open a copy of John le Carré's *Tinker, Tailor, Soldier Spy*. At the time I was fresh out of college. Smiley was much older, and had just been forcibly retired. By the time we met on page seventeen, I was no longer sure what planet I was on, but I was certain that the universe had changed forever. The planets had collided.

Part of it was that Smiley himself was a different kind of hero — "small, podgy, and at best middle-aged, he was by appearance one of London's meek who do not inherit the earth." Later, of course, Smiley revealed his strengths as we watched him probe and question, ever the gentlemen, yet possessing an intellectual ruthlessness that could wound more deeply than a dagger.

But even more impressive was Smiley's supporting cast, not just the bunch working down at the Circus – le Carré's slang for British intelligence — but everyone on every page, right down to the bit part schoolboys.

One after the other, le Carré nailed them with a few artful sentences. I didn't just picture them, I knew them — their foibles and anxieties, yearnings and motives. It was a Dickensian feast of nobs and wretches, often with strangely apt names (could a boss named Percy Alleline be anything other than a twit?)

It wasn't always easy following what they were up to. They talked in their own language, whether it was prep school argot or the jargon of spycraft. But that was part of the charm.

There were other attractions, too — the exotic locales, the onion skin plot, the gray-upon-gray morality with its dodgy choices and bleak rationalizations, and, of course, the elegant and knowing prose.

From my current vantage point, it seems painfully naïve to state that even so-called genre fiction can aspire to literary glory. Yet, in those days, fresh from the heirarchy of Lit classes and textbooks, it felt like a revelation, and changed forever what I would aspire to as both a reader and a writer.

Around age 30 I had the pleasure of meeting le Carré — David Cornwell, as he is properly known — during his visit to Baltimore for a university lecture. I was one of three journalists who shared the privilege of a lengthy interview. That's when I learned the nature of Smiley's birth. Cornwell created him in longhand on a legal pad during commuter rides on a London train.

That, too, was an inspiration, to hear of such a humble beginning from this author who spoke as well as he wrote — in full paragraphs, every clause perfectly balanced. And it was a pleasant reminder of that moment way back on page seventeen, when George Smiley walked into my world and changed it forever.

Dan Fesperman's fourth novel, *The Prisoner of Guantánamo*, was published in July 2006. Two of his previous books won

Dagger awards from the British Crime Writers' Association. A former foreign correspondent for The Sun, he lives in Baltimore with his wife, Liz Bowie, and their two children.

Sandra Tooley on
Salem's Lot by Stephen King (1975)

Work was boring in my teens. Stocking shelves in an office supply store taught me a life lesson in what I didn't want to do when I grew up. Lunch hours were my only escape as I sat on boxes between shelves in the back room eating my sandwich.

To my surprise, stocked in the back room were volumes of Nancy Drew books. The prelude to today's ditsy blonde, Nancy stumbled onto more crimes than Jessica Fletcher. I easily flew through one book each lunch hour. These books were my first taste of the puzzle, the whodunit, the why.

While immersing myself in mysteries, I encountered a strange detour. My cousin, being a voracious reader herself, tossed a copy of *Salem's Lot* in my lap and my bookshelves haven't looked the same since. It brought to life every delicious fear I had as a child. Stephen King's classic horror novel focused on Ben Mears, a writer, who returns to his hometown of Jerusalem's Lot to discover things aren't quite right. He bonds with eleven-year-old Mark Petrie who is curious about the new resident living in the Marsden House. From the moment he stepped into the Marsden House, I became that kid. I became Mark Petrie. I felt his fear as he climbed the darkened stairs. My heart pounded along with his and the clammy sweat in his palms were transferred to mine.

Salem's Lot contained all the elements I loved in a mystery — the crime, the clues, the good guy and the not-so-good guy doing evil deeds. King explored the boundaries of good and evil and the extent people would go to fulfill their objectives. The killer in *Salem's Lot* wasn't following the rules of How to Kill/ Maim/Terrorize 101. He didn't resemble your everyday villain found in a traditional mystery novel. In *Salem's Lot,* I found my fear and anticipation ratcheted up several notches. King transported the reader into another realm, asking that you leave all reality and expectations at the door and just fasten your seat belt. Of course, we know vampires don't exist…but the true skill of a storyteller is that he makes you believe it's possible. If this weren't true, then why did so many readers of *Salem's Lot* sleep with their lights on?

I found myself straddling the make-believe world King painted and traditional mysteries. As a writer I thought, why should I have to choose? Why limit myself to traditional mysteries when there are so many facets of the imagination to explore? Mysteries propel readers into a fictional world for hours of entertainment. Stretching one's imagination could be just as entertaining. Why couldn't I combine reality with elements of the unbelievable, whether it was the crime that overstepped the boundaries or the hero/heroine using extraordinary abilities to solve the crime?

I edged into my world cautiously, careful to include all the elements of a mystery while satisfying my King-ism by combining crimes that asked, "how the hell did they do that?" with characters possessing talents we wish we had, solving cases we sometimes hope to never face.

Salem's Lot has a special place on my bookshelf. The cover is tattered, its pages dog-eared and yellowed. I have reread *Salem's Lot* too many times to count and still sleep with the lights on.

Oh … and I currently work part-time at a retail store, stocking shelves.

Sandra Tooley, the author of six published novels and three short stories, has twice won ForeWord Magazine's Book of the

Year Award and was a finalist for the 2004 Derringer Award. *The Unseen*, her third Chase Dagger mystery written as Lee Driver, won the 2005 IPPY Award.

Ed Gorman on
Buyer Beware by John Lutz (1976)

Norman Mailer once described fellow writer Nelson Algren as the Grand Oddball and I think you'd have to say something similar about John Lutz's greatest creation, Alo Nudger. Nudger also happens to be, for me, one of most fully realized of all the private eyes who have ever trod the mean streets. The difference is that Nudger most likely treads these streets in Hush Puppies. Green Hush Puppies.

It would take half a page to list the various ways in which Nudger differs from his fellow fictional private eyes. Shall we speak of his car, the battered and bashed and dysfunctional VW; his constant consumption of antacid tablets; the time he spends in the donut shop on the ground floor below him (he hates their donuts, by the way); the way he relies on a cop buddy who treats him like a slightly stupid pet dog; the mid-life crisis that probably started when he was ten or so; the loneliness he tries to dispell by learning even more baseball trivia; and the endless crunching on those damned antacid tablets.

Alo might be the distant American cousin of Simon Brett's Charles Paris because both belong to the tradition of the serio-comic sufferer whose doggedness, occasional blind luck and soul-weary faith in the essential goodness of human beings keeps them running. Kevin Burton Smith has pointed out that one of Alo's best lines is "People shouldn't do this kind of thing to each other." Charles needs booze to keep going; Alo just requires those godawful donuts.

All these traits are on vivid, hilarious, heartbreaking display in the first Alo Nudger novel, *Buyer Beware*. The plot looks simple enough: Nudger getting hired to return a kidnapped child to her father. The problem is, the kidnapped child routine is a ruse, and soon enough Alo finds himself in mortal trouble, trouble so bad no amount of crunching antacids will help him.

Like all the Nudgers, *Buyer* is a quiet, elegiac study of losers good and bad. Lutz is never afraid to show us true evil, but he does so with restraint and a tendency to find the bad guys occasionally just as inept as Alo himself. In Alo's world there is definitely a God looking down upon the human circus, but you suspect He's just as melancholy as we are. It's this sense that makes the Nudgers some of the finest detective fiction of my generation.

Join Alo as he treads the mean streets in his green Hush Puppies. He's a lot of fun. Just don't try those donuts.

Ed Gorman has published 23 novels and six collections of short stories in a variety of genres over the past quarter century. Two of his books are in pre-production as films and one of his short stories was used as a one-act play, currently being performed.

M.J. Rose on
A Judgement in Stone by Ruth Rendell (1977)

"I would think that the old-fashioned detective story which is so much a matter of clues and puzzles, is certainly on the way out, if not already gone. Crime novels now are much more novels of character, and novels which look at the world we live in." (Interview in The Irish Times.)

In the 1980s, when I was the creative director of a mid-sized New York City advertising agency, my childhood dream of being a novelist went from a burning desire to a barely flickering flame. I'd always wanted to be a writer, but I was no longer sure I wanted to write. Everything I was reading about plot, about language, about narration, about voice, left out what fascinated me most: the psychology of the characters.

The more books I read and the more writers I met, the more I became convinced that if I wanted to pursue an alternative career, it shouldn't be that of a author, but rather a psychologist.

And then, in 1988, on a flight to LA to shoot a commercial, I started reading *A Judgement in Stone* by Ruth Rendell.

"Eunice Parchman Killed the Coverdale family because she could not read or write."

Rendell had me with the first line and hasn't let me go for the last twenty years. But it's not the quality of that initial book that impacted me — I'd been reading great and good and bad books for years.

Like a first kiss, *Judgement in Stone* opened my eyes to what was possible. It was the first true novel of psychological suspense I'd read by a contemporary writer (even if it wasn't yet categorized as such) and it rekindled my dream.

Yes, in *Judgment in Stone*, Rendell writes stunning descriptions and brilliant dialog, creates a complex plot and pays immaculate attention to detail. But it's her ability to take readers deeper and deeper into her character's psyche that makes her the master she is and makes *Judgment in Stone* such a seminal book both in her oeuvre and for me.

Today it's hard to realize that in the '70s, when Rendell wrote this book, it was controversial that on the first page not only the murder but the murderer's identity is given away.

This was no ordinary whodunit — it was a whydunit. The mystery is not who committed this crime but rather — why was this crime committed?

And that was a radical departure.

No less stunning was how Rendell created a pageturner and yet at the same time wrote a book that indicted society for turning a blind eye to the problems of illiteracy in England.

It's a novel of depth, of psychology, of sociology, of ideas.

"I'm more interested in the motivation than the crime itself," Rendell said in a 2002 interview in The Age. "I am fascinated by what makes people do dreadful things, not by how they do them."

And for this reader and writer, that fascination opened up a world of possibility.

Judgement in Stone became my talisman, reminding me that labels and genre descriptions only exist to be stretched and twisted and turned inside out until you find your own balance of hide and seek, internal and external, and dark and light.

M.J. Rose (www.mjrose.com) is the author of several novels of psychological suspense including *The Halo Effect,* which was an nominated for an Anthony Award. Her most recent novel is *The Venus Fix* (2006). Her work has also appeared in Oprah Magazine, Poets & Writers and several anthologies. Rose runs two popular blogs, Backstory and Buzz, Balls & Hype.

Joanne Pence on
Compromising Positions by Susan Isaacs (1978)

I thought dentists were bad until I encountered periodontists. I should have known they were evil incarnate when I was warned that if I ever needed my gums worked on, to get my whole mouth done at once because most people who had only half their mouths torn apart never went back to complete the job.

It was after an encounter with one of the supposed top practitioners of that profession that I began to read Susan Isaacs' *Compromising Positions.* When I read that Dr. M. Bruce Fleckstein had "shot his final wad of novacaine, probed his ultimate gum," I was hooked.

Before coming across this book, which was published in 1978, my mystery reading had consisted mainly of Christie, Sayers, Chandler, Ross Macdonald and Rex Stout. Although movies were having fun with the detective/mystery genre — from *The Thin Man* to comedies like Goldie Hawn's *Foul Play* (one of my favorites), my mystery reading remained serious until *Compromising Positions*.

For the first time, I came across an American housewife amateur sleuth who was smart, witty, scared, and very, very funny. What I especially liked about Judith Bernstein Singer was that she had a life — such a full life that the murder itself took back stage. Now, this isn't necessarily a good thing in a murder mystery, but *Compromising Positions* wasn't published as a mystery per se. (Today, it probably would have been.) But almost 30 years ago, we wouldn't expect a mystery to open on Valentine's Day with our sleuth's finger tracing hearts pierced with non-lethal arrows on frosted kitchen windows while waiting for her husband. We wouldn't see her give that husband a Valentine's Day present that he leaves unopened, or see them eat dinner, or see him going upstairs afterward for their three-times a week "quickie." Isaacs lets us see the problem in this marriage right away:

"I'll meet you upstairs," he said, giving me his knowing look. "Hurry up with the dishes."
I worked slowly, patiently scraping the gristle and remaining green beans into the garbage...

This, I thought, is what I want to write. Something about real people — rich, that's okay — but in real-life, everyday situations that I could understand on some deep level beyond the terror, gore and finality of murder. Love, sex and the meaningfulness of a housewife's life were at the heart of Isaacs' book, all wrapped up in a neat murder-mystery package.

It was like finding a little bit of heaven.

Throw in a sexy cop for added interest — Lt. Nelson Sharpe might have been short and gray-haired, but he reeked sex appeal and danger. My own series heroine, Angie Amalfi, chased the cop she loved, San Francisco Homicide Inspector Paavo Smith, for ten books before getting him to propose. Cops can be mysterious, elusive, but definitely sexy, in uniform or out.

Having an amateur sleuth housewife insinuate herself into the lives of her neighbors wasn't a new notion by any means, but that it was done with such humor — a pornography-pushing periodontist who enticed rich married housewives with second-rate lunches at Wong Foo's as the victim; a dim-witted Dicky Dunck as a prime suspect — and placed in the middle of a world that readers could look at with both fascination, envy and a little distaste (*"I cannot seem to comprehend the meaning of these flawless women, why they're here."*), Isaacs lets us see the yearning her sleuth has for something more, and the effect on her staid life as she closes in on the murderer.

Angie Amalfi is my rich, ethnic sleuth, and from the time she meets Inspector Paavo Smith, she's in a world that is completely new and infinitely exciting to her. Food, humor and romance are a part of her world as well — and she owes it all to Susan Isaacs.

Joanne Pence writes the Angie Amalfi mystery series, and has written romantic suspense, short stories and a novella. A USA Today and Independent Mystery Bookstore Association bestseller, she has worked as a journalist and government analyst, and now lives in Idaho with her family. *Red Hot Murder* is her latest mystery.

Elizabeth Gunn on
The Empty Copper Sea by John D. MacDonald (1978)

When I was an innkeeper in Helena, Montana, I used to pass slow hours on the late shift reading John D. MacDonald's Travis McGee mysteries. McGee lived in Florida on a sybaritic houseboat called "The Busted Flush," and made his living finding things for people who couldn't, or wouldn't, use the usual channels. His fees were simplicity itself: McGee kept half of whatever he found. His methods were a tad short of legal, but his moral code allowed him to skip lightly over gray areas and land on the square marked, "Good." His sidekick was Meyer, a brilliant economist on a boat called the "John Maynard Keynes," who, like McGee, made quiet money on the dodgy fringes. McGee had a memorable tan, an affinity for Boodles gin, great fishing skills and remarkable success with lissome beauties in bikinis.

Literary critics sometimes complained that MacDonald's women were two-dimensional, his attitudes tended toward male chauvinism and his plots were formulaic. But they weren't standing where I was, watching the next blizzard come over Mount Helena and waiting in vain for the last five customers to come in and make my day. Like legions of other pale-skinned MacDonald fans shivering in down-filled coats, I knew MacDonald had my number and I didn't care. McGee was cool, his stories were too exciting to put down, and I wanted his life and his boat.

This is not a cautionary tale. In fact the burden of my story is, do not be careful what you wish for. Some years after my first flirtation with Travis, my husband and I sold our motels, drove to San Diego and bought a sailboat. By some fluke of extraordinary luck, we sailed it to Mexico and back in the next year and a half, did not drown or sink the vessel, and became citizens of the world. After that voyage, we wandered the earth and seas in a succession of boats, planes and RVs, coming to rest at last in the Florida Keys with a nice trawler, in which we navigated the eastern seaboard and the Bahamas for six adventurous years. MacDonald didn't lie; living on a boat in Florida is cool.

We never retrieved any suspect loot for anybody, but we discovered the glorious treasure of the life under the sea, and my husband brought all that beauty back on board in his camera. I found the courage to write that I'd been looking for all my life, and the Jake Hines mystery series was born.

The irony is, my hero's not a sailor. He's a police detective in a mid-size town in Southeast Minnesota, and lives in an old farmhouse halfway between his town and Saint Paul, where his smart, sexy lover is a forensic scientist at the state crime lab. The Jake Hines novels — six so far — go back to where I was born and include the best of everything I've learned since and am still learning.

I try never to forget the lessons MacDonald has to teach a writer: set the hook early, keep the story moving and above all write about characters that interest you. Thousands of readers who can't recall MacDonald's plot twists have vivid, precise memories about the people and boats in the Travis McGee stories. That's the dream future that keeps writers bent over keyboards while their carefree friends play volleyball in the sunshine. We all imagine that one of these days we'll write a book you can never forget, the one achievement we can think of that's worth all the hard labor it requires.

Elizabeth Gunn writes the Jake Hines mystery series, police procedurals set in Southeast Minnesota where she grew up. Her latest, *Crazy Eights*, explores how drug traffic fractures families and cuts across class lines. She lives in Tucson and climbs mountains for fun.

J.A. Konrath on
The Judas Goat by Robert B. Parker (1978)

The year was 1979. I was in the fifth grade, nose-deep in the young adult works of Judy Blume and Beverly Cleary, when the unthinkable occurred.

I ran out of books.

It was a Saturday, raining like crazy outside, and my mom refused to drive me to the library, no matter how much I whined.

"You're almost a grown-up," she said, to placate me. "Why don't you start reading grown-up books?"

Mom had a point. The YA stuff had lost much of its edge. I was ready to read at a more mature level. After all, at nine-years-old I was practically an adult. I even had underarm hair. Two of them.

So I went to Mom's bookcase, filled with paperbacks by writers I'd never heard of. Agatha Christie. Dorothy Sayers. Ngaio Marsh. Ed McBain. John D. MacDonald. And Robert B. Parker.

Parker had the distinction of having the slimmest book on Mom's shelf. It was called *The Judas Goat*. For the three folks on the planet who aren't familiar with Parker, he writes about a Boston private eye named Spenser, an ex-boxer with a penchant for wisecracks. Spenser has a lethal sidekick named Hawk, a bald black man who works as a mob enforcer.

It was quite the eye-opener, going from Ramona the Pest to Spenser and Hawk. By the end of the book, my eyes were as big as my head. The duo had to stop a 350-pound Russian weightlifter named Zachery, and the finale involves a ten-page fist fight where they keep trying to knock the big man down.

For a nine-year-old, it was the coolest thing ever put on paper. It sure made *Tales of a Fourth Grade Nothing* seem lame. Who knew writing could be so cool? Who knew a book could be more exciting than anything ever on television?

Apparently, Parker knew. And after reading him, I did too.

So began my love affair with mysteries. I read all of Parker, and then moved on to other authors, eventually amassing a mystery book collection of over 5000 titles.

But I'll never forget my first love. *The Judas Goat* was one of those defining moments for me. By the end of that book, I knew what I wanted to be when I grew up: a bald black mob enforcer.

That didn't turn out as I'd hoped, so I became a writer instead.

The reverberations from *The Judas Goat* lingered for many years. Savvy readers of my first novel, *Whiskey Sour*, might remember a scene in a bar where my hero, Jack Daniels, and her bald mob-enforcer sidekick, get into an extended fist fight with a 350-pound guy where they keep trying to knock the big man down. This is an homage (which is French and means "rip-off") of Robert B. Parker's *The Judas Goat*.

I'm eternally grateful for Parker's book. I'm grateful for his witty dialog. I'm grateful for his slam-bang action. I'm grateful for his clever plot. But most of all, I'm grateful for his book being slim. If *Murder on the Orient Express* had been a bit shorter, I'd be writing cozies for a living.

J.A. Konrath (www.JAKonrath.com) is the author of several thrillers in the Lt. Jack Daniels series: *Rusty Nail*, *Whisky Sour* and *Bloody Mary*. His work has appeared in many magazines and anthologies, including Ellery Queen, Alfred Hitchcock, The Strand and *Thriller* edited by James Patterson.

Toni L.P. Kelner on
The Tightrope Walker by Dorothy Gilman (1979)

Ever since I learned to read, I've been a bookworm, happily

devouring stories about other places, other times, other worlds, other people. Especially other people. I fell in love with countless characters: from brilliant Sherlock Holmes to feisty Trixie Belden and intrepid Nancy Drew, from mysterious Gandalf to dashing Robin Hood, from smart-assed Archie Goodwin to unfailingly polite Peter Wimsey. All those perfectly wonderful characters were so different from anybody I knew, and so different from me. That is, until I met Amelia Jones in Dorothy Gilman's *The Tightrope Walker.*

Amelia was shy and painfully unsure of herself. She wasn't particularly attractive or well-built, and she was inexperienced with men. She didn't see herself as having any talent worth sharing with the world, and had no driving ambition. Her main solace seemed to be in books. In other words, she was me! I recognized myself just from the first two sentences in the book:

Maybe everyone lives with terror every minute of the every day and buries it, never stopping long enough to look. Or maybe it's just me.

It wasn't just Amelia — it was me, too — and it's hard to explain how much it affected me to find someone so much like myself on the pages of a book. As I read about her adventures in tracking down and escaping from a murderer, I kept thinking that if she could do that, maybe I could, too. Of course, I wasn't likely to encounter a murderer, but in addition to the mystery plot, Amelia found a job that interested her, made friends and a home for herself, and fell in love. Again, if she could do it, so could I.

I know it sounds as if Gilman inspired me more as a person than as a writer, but she did both. Even before I read *The Tightrope Walker,* I'd been trying to write, and like a lot of new writers, I concocted stories with perfected versions of myself as the heroine, making myself thinner, taller, smarter, braver, stronger and better-dressed. Unsurprisingly, these "perfect" heroines were as lively as a fence post, and since they were already perfect before their stories started, the plots were boring, too. I could have given those characters some of my weaknesses, maybe even some of my strengths, but I didn't think that anybody would want to read about me. Now Dorothy Gilman had written a book about somebody like me, and it had been published. Once again, I thought that if she could do that, I could, too.

So while I based Laura Fleming, the protagonist of my first mystery series, loosely on myself, she isn't a flawless reflection. I gave her family relationships that aren't always comfortable. I made her impatient and frequently cranky. I gave her prejudices and blind spots. Okay, I did make her taller and thinner than I am, but I most definitely did not make her perfect. I'd learned that perfect characters aren't fun to read, and certainly no fun to write.

Writing about a version of myself also helped me learn how to create characters who are nothing like me: a old Jewish man who runs a convenience store, an elephant trainer, a small-town police chief, a woman who sells lingerie, even a carny. The only thing they have in common is the fact that they aren't perfect either.

One last thought. Before I wrote this essay, I reread my copy of *The Tightrope Walker* for the first time in many years, and I was delighted to find that it's still a perfectly wonderful book. I was just as delighted to realize that I'm not much like Amelia Jones anymore.

Toni L.P. Kelner has published eight mystery novels, and numerous short stories. *Without Mercy*, the first in her "Where Are They Now?" series, is planned for release in 2007. Kelner lives just north of Boston, Massachusetts, with her two daughters and husband, fellow writer Stephen P. Kelner, Jr.

Beverle Graves Myers on
The Name of the Rose by Umberto Eco (1983)

In this weighty historical mystery, author Umberto Eco gives us a medieval Sherlock Holmes and an adolescent Watson ferreting out the truth behind a series of murders in a Benedictine abbey. I first became acquainted with William of Baskerville and Adso of Melk after the release of the English translation in 1983. Like many readers, I was amazed at Eco's erudition, but it wasn't the detailed theological debates that stayed with me. When I embarked on writing my own historical mystery, I went back to *The Name of the Rose* to study the techniques Eco used to bring the abbey and its inhabitants so vividly to life.

My chosen milieu was eighteenth-century Venice. History books told me that the shrinking maritime empire was on the brink of economic collapse and had staved off the inevitable by reinventing herself as the pleasure capital of Europe. *Carnevale* reigned six months of the year, masquerade was the order of the day, and all levels of society met and mingled at the opera houses that had become the focus of theatrical entertainment. So far, so good. But it would take more than bare facts to draw readers into that glittering era. Eco showed me the way.

Each scene in the Rose's isolated abbey is drenched in sensory stimuli. The visual description is stunning: blood-stained snow surrounding the pigsty where a monk has been thrust headfirst into a vat of blood, a lake of milk-white fog covering the valley below the abbey. Our other senses are addressed just as strongly. We can feel the smoothness of a vellum page scraped with a pumice stone and softened with chalk to await the first touch of a scribe's pen. A cloud of dust and mildew arising from an ancient book tickles our noses.

Nor does Eco slight character development. A medieval monk who wears a tonsure and habit but speaks and acts like Joe Six-Pack isn't going to fool today's discriminating reader. Eco presents William of Baskerville with playful allusions to Sherlock Holmes — besides the obvious name, William chews a soporific herb when he wants to withdraw from the world — but this monk is very much a man of his time. Following the tenets of Roger Bacon and William of Occam, he attacks the puzzle of the murdered Benedictines with the logical reasoning of English Scholasticism. Of course, the mindset of an era is not confined to one way of thinking. William of Baskerville's shining light of reason is in danger of being extinguished by the dark superstitions and prejudices of other monks who are quick to hurl accusations of heresy at anyone who challenges their self-serving beliefs. Not an idle threat in the days of the Inquisition.

Unfortunately, the wealth of background in many passages serves as a double-edged sword. Detail can help immerse us in the fourteenth century, but sometimes I found myself wishing Eco had given us the condensed version. The political jousting between the Emperor and the Pope and how the rise of a monetary economy affects both is interesting, but contributes little to the plot. The same could be said for the wealth of detail on medieval heresies.

That criticism aside, *The Name of the Rose* is well worth the effort for the historical mystery reader. And for the writer who aspires to create a similarly engaging past world, studying this granddaddy of the genre is a must.

Beverle Graves Myers (www.beverlegravesmyers.com) writes the Baroque Mystery series featuring castrato soprano Tito Amato as an eighteenth-century opera singer with a stellar talent for sleuthing. *Painted Veil* is her latest novel. Bev also writes short stories that have appeared in numerous magazines and anthologies.

Libby Fischer Hellmann on
Briarpatch by Ross Thomas (1984)

I'd already published three novels when I stumbled onto *Briarpatch* by Ross Thomas. When I started it, though, I instantly knew why I write the books I do. Simply put, *Briarpatch* has become one of the standards by which I measure the development of my own craft. Its structure, style and substance are an indispensable template, and its dog-eared pages and cracked spine will stay in my library forever.

Structure: Briarpatch is a structural chameleon. Technically, it's an amateur sleuth novel. Ben Dill, a Senate staffer in Washington, DC, journeys to an unnamed city to bury his sister, a homicide detective killed in a bomb explosion. While there, he intends to find out why she died. In short order, though, characters are introduced, complications mount, and by page 30 I wasn't sure whether I was reading a police procedural, a PI novel, or a thriller peopled by ambitious politicians, intelligence operatives and arms-dealing mercenaries. While the constantly shifting alliances, judicious disclosure of information, and ambiguous characters build suspense, *Briarpatch* also has the earmarks of a modern morality tale.

In the hands of a lesser talent, this complexity might be disastrous, but Thomas distills the essence of each thread and weaves them into a seamless, satisfying story. I write an amateur sleuth series as well, and my plots often spill over from "traditional mystery" to thriller. I continue to learn from his example.

Style: Thomas's prose — spare, lucid, silky — is just this side of Chandler. It has rhythm. And pace. And while it's easy to read, it's never dull. Sometimes he breaks the rules, having fun at alliteration, for example, or planting his tongue firmly in his cheek. But the writing is never offensive, and a too clever sentence is redeemed in the next with a thoughtful observation.

Furthermore, *Briarpatch* illustrates the lessons we fiction writers learn: Show don't tell. Less is more. Thomas respects his readers enough to make us to work to add emotional and moral shadings. I came away from *Briarpatch* thinking Thomas says what he means and yet it means so much more.

Substance: I grew up in Washington, DC, and when my family gossiped about the neighbors, we were essentially talking politics. As a result, stories that touch on national or global issues draw me like a moth to the light. Fold in suspense, three-dimensional characters and a dark brooding story, and I'm sold.

Briarpatch delivers. Essentially it's a tale of murder, politics and corruption in a small town with tentacles that stretch to the nation's capital. (I learned after I read *Briarpatch* that Thomas lived in DC as well.)

It's not insignificant that Thomas teases us with the setting. We never know the city where *Briarpatch* takes place. We don't need to. It could be any town in which an ambitious police chief hungers for higher office, another policeman may be on the take, a former dirt-poor pal is now a millionaire, and a shady businessman tries to set up his former partner. Indeed, the pretense of Southern civility coupled with the raw pursuit of power is reminiscent of *All the King's Men* — perhaps the best American political novel ever written.

But perhaps the novel's most attractive — and durable — quality is that it's a story lightly told. *Briarpatch* never screams or calls attention to itself. Like a fine wine, its subtle complexity sneaks up on you — until you realize you're in the hands of a master and you've been reading a classic.

Libby Fischer Hellmann writes the Anthony-nominated Chicago-based series featuring video producer and single mom Ellie Foreman. Her first novel was nominated for an Anthony, and her second for a Benjamin Franklin award. All four are published by Poisoned Pen Press and Berkley Prime Crime. Libby has served as Sisters in Crime President and President of MWA Midwest's chapter.

Julie A. Hyzy on
C is for Corpse by Sue Grafton (1986)

Little did Sue Grafton know, when she solicited questions on a book-tour luncheon in Chicago, that the first question she answered (mine) was asked less for the benefit of entertaining the audience and more for getting my own series off to a solid start.

At that luncheon at the Union League club, Grafton was promoting the latest in her alphabet series. I'd read every one of protagonist Kinsey Millhone's adventures from *A is for Alibi* through *Q is for Quarry*. But it was *C is for Corpse*, early on, that snagged me as a major mystery fan.

In *Corpse*, Kinsey takes on Bobby Callahan, a handsome young man recently disfigured and left handicapped by a car accident that he swears was a deliberate attempt on his life. Bobby hires Kinsey to find out who did it, but can't recall who's after him. Or why.

A few days later Bobby's dead and Kinsey decides that her client deserves his money's worth. She sets out to find the killer.

Kinsey's wry vision of the world, her eye for eccentric detail and her impressions of the people around her make every scene come to sparkling life. Grafton gives Kinsey a clear voice — like a tolling bell on a still summer morning — and readers can't help but stop and listen.

That's exactly what I hoped to emulate when I started my "Deadly" series. I didn't set out to recreate Kinsey — I wouldn't want to do that. What I attempted is that clarity of characterization at which Sue Grafton excels.

Kinsey is genuine. She jumps off the page and into the reader's life with verve. She sweats, she hurts, she delights in comfort food. And throughout, she leads readers on her whirl-wind adventures — adventures that keep us guessing, but that are so grounded in reality that when she triumphs at the end, we can't help but feel as though we're right there with her.

In *C is for Corpse*, the CFFL scene (Customary Fight For one's Life) is masterful. Like most avid readers I realize that since this is a first-person account and there are subsequent books in this series, Kinsey will survive. And yet, the setting — a deserted morgue at twilight, where the only living people are Kinsey and the murderer who's humming an old Gershwin tune — evokes the kind of chill that makes you want to make sure your doors and windows are locked.

My question at the Chicago luncheon event was this: "If you were to start your series today, what would you do differently?" I wanted to know because, to me, Sue Grafton had accomplished the near impossible. She'd brought a character to life who not only kept me entertained through seventeen novels, but who did so with believability — with energy. I couldn't imagine she'd made any missteps, but I wanted to hear what the author herself had to say. Grafton explained that if she were to do things differently, she might choose to keep a never-aging Kinsey current, rather than have her set in the 1980s.

Like a sponge I soaked up everything she said about her series and her writing style — delighted to have the opportunity to learn from the woman whose novels made me appreciate the adult mystery genre.

Back at my keyboard, I'm filled with ideas for future story arcs. Reading Sue Grafton's novels and then hearing her talk about them has had a profound influence on my writing. Like that clear summer bell, her words resonate with me as I dive in, each day, to create my own "Deadly" adventures.

Julie Hyzy is the author of *Artistic License*, a standalone romantic suspense, and of the Alex St. James mystery series, which includes *Deadly Blessings* and the forthcoming *Deadly Interest*. Julie's written several award-winning short stories and is currently working on a techno-thriller titled *Virtual Twilight*.

Jan Brogan on
Presumed Innocent by Scott Turow (1987)

When a friend lent me *Presumed Innocent* by Scott Turow, she marked a page less than a quarter way into the book. This, she explained, was the point at which she guessed who "did it."

But even with the page clearly marked, the ending wasn't revealed to me. From the very first page, I was so caught up with the tortured protagonist Rusty Sabich, so fascinated by his obsession with Carolyn Polhemus and whether it drove him to murder, that I paid no attention to any other clue. I didn't realize the question was who did it. All I wanted to know was whether Rusty could have done it.

Mysteries are about how far will people go to get what they want, and what lines they are willing to cross. But usually, these questions are focused on the antagonist and/or alternate suspects. In *Presumed Innocent*, Scott Turow twists the form by focusing the question of human weakness on the protagonist instead.

In all his books, Turow reveals a deep understanding of people and a great compassion for even the most minor character. I often feel as if I've long known these characters, and as if they are teaching me something completely new about humankind. But Rusty Sabich is the most complicated because of a fascinating contradiction: he is believable as a character, but not as a narrator.

In *Presumed Innocent*, there are the usual, external obstacles to solving the crime: Multiple suspects. Cops who lie. Evidence that disappears. But the biggest obstacle comes from within. A complicated and oddly sympathetic protagonist who cheated on his wife and may have murdered his girlfriend, Rusty Sabich has good reason to lie or block his recollection of the truth. Trying to decide whether to trust him or not kept me on the edge of my seat.

For that reason, when I started to write my first novel, *Final Copy*, I began with a flawed protagonist. Not superficially flawed, like the private investigators with commitment issues or the alcohol problems that are kept in check. I wanted to create a deeply flawed character, a protagonist whose quest for justice was complicated not just by external forces, but by her own inner demons.

I continued to favor the flawed character in the Hallie Ahern series. If the protagonist is smart, savvy and morally irreproachable, there isn't much anxiety. Of course he/she will overcome the external obstacles to solve the puzzle, reveal the truth and right all wrongs. But if the protagonist is like most of us, prone to a mistake or two and subject to emotion, the degree of difficulty increases and the suspense kicks up a notch. The reader stops trying to guess how justice will be served and starts to worry if justice will be served.

By making us wary of his protagonist from chapter to chapter, Turow created both suspense and misdirection, resulting in what I consider the perfect mystery. After I'd galloped to a conclusion both shocking and believable, I could see that Turow had played fair. Completely consumed with trying to decipher Rusty Sabich, I'd been blissfully ignorant of all the carefully laid clues.

Jan Brogan is the author of *Final Copy* (Larcom Press) and *A Confidential Source* (Mysterious Press). She is currently at work on the second in the Hallie Ahern series (St. Martin's Minotaur).

Colin Cotterill on
The Silence of the Lambs by Thomas Harris (1988)

I suppose I should credit that remarkable man Raji Patel for my becoming a writer of mysteries. Before you run off to look him up on the Internet, I have to tell you that Raji had a little open-air Indian restaurant beside the Vientiane Hospital in Laos. He ran it with his sister Violet. His specialty was dollops of food served on indented tin trays — brown atolls of mystery on a silver pond. I stopped off for a Raji special on a trip to the capital one day. I don't know if it was the heat or the exotic insects, but something about that meal left me laid up for a week in the room above Efi's frock shop.

Efi had two books. One was a searing romance between two muscle bound mustachioed Hell's Angels. The other was Thomas Harris' *The Silence of the Lambs*. I could see no point in reading either. Hell's Angel relationships always ended in tears, and I'd seen the *Lambs* movie in Bangkok the previous year. What possible pleasure could be derived from a thriller whose secrets had already been exposed to you? How could a written Dr. Hannibal Lecter be any more creepy and evil than Anthony Hopkins? How could Officer Clarice Starling in print be more vulnerable and downtrodden than Jody Foster on celluloid? But, believe me, after three days of diarrhea you'd read just about anything.

After *The Heat of My Saddle*, I turned to Harris, and I don't mind admitting he scared the bejeebers out of me. It made no difference that I knew what was around every corner. I still yelled, "Don't get in the back of that van, girl," and turned the page hoping this time she hadn't. I was astounded. It was a revelation to me that well-crafted prose could send me off into alleyways that were even eerier than those in the movies.

I have to confess here that I didn't use to be much of a reader. School didn't help in that regard. "Read this over the weekend and write a 400-word book report." If that didn't cure you of the reading habit... If it didn't have pictures it was work. By the time I reached 30, I was still mouthing the words and following them across the page with my finger. But something happened on that day over the frock shop. It was the literary equivalent of finding God. I experienced the power of the written word. It wasn't in the gore and the slaughter. Writers have been getting cheap thrills with large helpings of blood and entrails for years. It was in subtle things.

How could I have imagined, for example, what a wallop intelligence could pack? I was in Pakse training teachers and I'd always seen knowledge as a present: the great white seer passing on the secrets of the universe. But was I scaring my young teachers? Did they feel the same frightening force of intellect that Clarice suffered in dialogues with the cannibal? He wasn't frightening because he bit off people's faces (although that probably helped), he was an ogre because he was smart. I'd always felt that people who knew more than me were annoying, but I'd never imagined harnessing that vexation and turning it into power. Harris' words did that and much more. I set off on a quest to find the secret of weaving magic in print. I wanted to scare the life out of people, and marry them to characters the way Thomas Harris did. Some hope.

Colin Cotterill (www.colincotterill.com) was born in London in 1952. He taught teachers in Thailand and Laos before becoming involved in child protection in the region. He's also a cartoonist and writer. His third novel in the Dr. Siri series, *Disco for the Departed,* will be released by Soho Press in 2006. He lives in Chiangmai.

Phil Dunlap on
A Thief of Time by Tony Hillerman (1988)

By an early age, I learned that reading was a way of life, not just a source of short-term entertainment. I not only reveled in the written word, but also found my love of writing followed a natural progression to emulate what I'd read, to give my own created characters life as others had done for my enjoyment. As I got older, G. K. Chesterton intrigued me with his stories of mystery, widening a youthful interest in solving crime. But I also have long been a fan of western history and literature, primarily late nineteenth century tales of gunfighters and out-laws, cattle drives and cowboy justice. I was drawn to the pure "right versus wrong" aspects of law and order, of lawmen turned bad, and of vigilante justice.

Nearly all of my fiction writing as an adult had been of one genre or the other. But it was Tony Hillerman who showed me how the West is timeless, strange and wondrous, and also a place in which mysteries are right at home. That's when the light went on. For me, it became a logical transition to tie my two greatest loves together, mystery and the Old West. The course was charted that would eventually see my first book being sold.

Exactly what was it about Hillerman's novels that made me look at my own writing differently? In a word: smooth. His novels let me read at a pace reminiscent of wandering through an uncharted wilderness, thoughtfully poking and probing, instead of making me feel as if I was being driven to a rock concert in a speeding dune buggy (as so many authors today feel they must do). He drew me into the lives of his characters as easily as meeting long lost family. We spent enjoyable hours together, and I found a way to tiptoe around the traditional shoot-em-up.

In *A Thief of Time*, said by many to be Hillerman's best

effort, Lt. Joe Leaphorn and Sgt. Jim Chee investigate criminals who are raiding ancient burial grounds, resulting in the theft of priceless artifacts sacred to the Navajo Nation. As I read his novels, I learn much about Indian culture, both past and present, the characters, the everyday lives of a people who are every bit a part of modern America, yet quite apart from the way of life in which I was brought up. They drive cars, go to work each day and fall in love, while at the same time managing to survive constant threats to life (both natural and man-made), pursue evildoers and triumph over crime — albeit at a less-than-frenetic pace. And the best part is that these unassuming Navajo policemen manage to remain firmly immersed in their own ancient culture, surrounded by spirit beings, ghosts, shamans and ritual ceremonies. Hillerman's world is full of the past, the present, and the unknown, all of which have made me a fervent follower, and been an inspiration to my own writings.

Because my western mysteries are set in the nineteenth century, I, too, find comfort using the land itself as both protagonist and antagonist, allowing my characters to become a part of the social and economic landscape, just as Hillerman does in his modern-day western mysteries. His descriptions of life in an arid desert, mixed with his unique style of writing, which accurately emulate the heartbeat of the Navajo Nation, have been an inspiration to me as I attempt to draw water from an analogous well. Do not presume that I pretend to compare my own writing to that of a classic writer like Tony Hillerman, but I can strive, can't I?

Phil Dunlap's first novel, *The Death of the Desert Belle*, was published by Avalon Books in 2004. It is a nineteenth century police procedural. His second book, closer to a pure western, though still containing those elements of mystery, is *Call of the Gun* (Avalon, 2005). In addition to his books, Phil has been published in magazines and newspapers for nearly 20 years.

Harley Jane Kozak on
The Eight by Katherine Neville (1988)

Is *The Eight* a classic? As classics go, Katherine Neville's book hasn't been around all that long. I found it the year it came out in paperback, 1990. Like the novel's heroine, I was young, independent and working in an interesting field. I lived alone in a big city. I traveled a lot. I had no responsibilities to anything but the pursuit of art, politics, religion, romance, the ten-minute mile and the meaning of life.

I picked up *The Eight* in a bookstore, attracted by the title and the cover, and it was love at first chapter. It's a tricky book to describe. I found myself buying copies and handing them to friends, which was easier than saying, "Well, it's a mystery, and a thriller, it takes place in 1972 and 1792, but it's really a love story, a New York story, a Paris story, a story of Algiers, with math and chess pieces and politics, the French Revolution and the Cold War, magic, mysticism, espionage, religion, philosophy, friendships, nuns, couture, art and pop culture; plus madness, mayhem, murder and really bad skin disease."

And intelligence. Its heroines were smart. Not that popular fiction has ever lacked smart women, but in *The Eight*, intelligence was no mere fashion accessory, an accompaniment to long legs and a Glock in the Fendi handbag; these girls had the kind of brains that fueled the plot. They were extravagantly smart. Unapologetically smart. Eruditely smart. The men were smart too. I went to bed happy that the world was populated by so many intelligent people.

I assured my friends, however, that it was really just entertainment. Escapist fare. I emphasized this point, as some had not yet recovered from the Christmas I gave out copies of *The Second Sex*. In fact, *The Eight* was a beach book. A North African beach book. And a feminist beach book, populated with such powerful women as Catherine the Great, Charlotte Corday and Madame de Stael, but I may have left them out of the description. I might also have neglected to mention OPEC, the international chess scene, economic theory, mathematical formulae, quantum physics, symmetry, synchronicity, serendipity and the Fibonacci numbers. Happily, there were enough descriptions of food, restaurants, sweaty sex, and what everyone was or wasn't wearing to satisfy the most populist palate.

If the genre was hard to pin down, so was the story, told as it was in flashbacks within flashbacks, shifting centuries and points of view, plot points in fables wrapped in enigmas wrapped in someone's grandmother's secrets hidden in the private lives of actual historical figures. (Napoleon! Charlemagne! George Washington!)

I believe the books that grab us and hold us captive are linked to the moment in our lives when we read them. The coming of age story we discover at adolescence, the literature that gets us through grief, heartache, homesickness, breaking through our defenses when actual people cannot. I have read books that challenged me, books that inspired me, books that left me breathless and frightened and unhinged, but *The Eight* was a book that found me in the midst of one career, and by some alchemical process, set me on the path of another. It's the book that made me want to write books. And how classic is that?

Harley Jane Kozak attended New York University's Graduate Acting Program, and spent three decades in stage, film and television. She's written *Dating Dead Men* and *Dating is Murder*, won the Agatha, Anthony and Macavity Awards, and had short fiction in *Ms. Magazine* and the anthology *This IS Chick Lit.* Harley lives in LA with her husband, two dogs and three children.

Carolyn Haines on
Black Cherry Blues by James Lee Burke (1989)

Heat lightning shimmered on the edge of the Crescent City when I stumbled into a bookseller's booth at a literary festival in New Orleans. The humidity was oppressive, suffocating even my love of books, as I picked up a paperback called *Black Cherry Blues*. Standing in the heat, thunderclouds building to the west, I read the opening pages, a dream sequence about the brutal murder of Annie Robicheaux. I paid for the book and took it back to my room, riveted by the wounded character of Dave Robicheaux and the descriptions of New Iberia, Louisiana.

Mysteries have always been my favorite genre to read. Like so many others of my generation, Nancy Drew and the Hardy Boys helped me create my own imaginary adventures of sleuthing and solving crimes in my hometown of Lucedale, Mississippi. I fell in love with the language of Edgar Allan Poe and his ability to evoke that tingle of delicious horror with his macabre tales.

I have great admiration for a number of mystery authors today, but it was Burke's *Black Cherry Blues* that struck me like one of his Louisiana lightning bolts, illuminating the powerful potential of a mystery story told with such mastery of language.

Burke's Robicheaux is a gravely flawed character, but one who struggles nobly against his own weaknesses. Robicheaux's violence is perfectly mirrored in the setting of a part of the country that still holds mysterious secrets.

The opening of *Black Cherry Blues*:

Her hair is curly and gold on the pillow, her skin white in the heat lightning that trembles beyond the pecan trees outside the bedroom window. The night is hot and breathless, the clouds painted like horsetails against the sky; a peal of thunder rumbles out on the Gulf like an apple rolling around in the bottom of a wood barrel, and the first raindrops ping against the window fan.

The image of Annie, asleep, is crystal clear. The violence to come foreshadowed by the weather.

Burke is a master of setting and character. My connection to his work is visceral. Sitting in my hotel room in New Orleans, I was transported beyond the boundaries of New Orleans and into a land of cypress swamps and danger. I was pulled so deeply into the story that I didn't want to surface, and I realized that was a goal I aspired to as a writer — to marry character, setting, theme and language to a finely crafted plot in a way that transported a reader.

Carolyn Haines is the author of the Sarah Booth Delaney Mississippi Delta mystery series. *Bones to Pick* was released in July 2006. *Judas Burning* (2005) and *Penumbra* (2006) are darker crime novels. All are set in her homeland of the South. Haines is a past recipient of an Alabama State Council of the Arts writing fellowship. She is active in animal rescue.

Tim Cockey on
Time's Witness by Michael Malone (1989)

There I was, minding my own business. Though in fact, I guess you could say I was minding the business of an author I'd been looking forward to reading. Which is to say, I was reading his book. If a book isn't its author's business, then I don't know what is.

I have to travel back to the early '90s to pull this memory out of the hat. I had moved from my native Baltimore to Chapel Hill, with the express purpose of investigating whether my lifelong dream of writing a novel was destined to remain a dream or to become, at long last, tangible. The goal was simple. I was not going to budge from that charming little college town until I had produced a novel — good, bad or indifferent. I wanted the *pages*, damn it. I wanted to see what would happen when I finally applied myself on a regular basis, a daily writing regimen.

All set. The Great-or-Not-So-Great American Novel was about to be attempted.

And then I read *Time's Witness* by Michael Malone. Credit the New York Times Sunday Book Review, where I'd come across a review of Malone's novel. Soon after moving to Chapel Hill, I came across a copy of the book. Came a nice sunny day and I pulled my shabby lounge chair up to the edge of the woods outside my cozy Carolina shack and cracked open *Time's Witness*.

Little did I know, I was cracking open the mystery writer within me.

It's a wonderful book. I don't even want to say, "it's a wonderful mystery." Have we ever heard anyone categorize *To Kill as Mockingbird* as "a wonderful courtroom drama?" It is that, of course. And of course it is so much more as well.

That's how things stand with *Time's Witness*. There is plenty of mystery. The brother of a young black man whose execution on murder charges has been temporarily stayed is murdered the day after the execution was to have taken place. Why? And what of the man on Death Row? Is he guilty or innocent? Eventually, we also get ourselves a nifty courtroom drama as well.

And what else do we get? We get a stunningly rendered cast of characters. We get a narrator of uncommon charm and common faults, Cuddy Mangum, the police chief of Hillston, North Carolina. We get a man who is dedicated to his role as chief law enforcement officer and also torn in his role as plain old flawed human with a very large broken heart. The object of his emotional solitude is the wife of the charismatic state senator, whose hands become increasingly dirty as the story moves along.

But that's all plot. And that's all fine. What Malone pulls off in this book is enviable beyond belief. The fabric of the community of Hillston and the surrounding area is perfectly rendered. The nuances of the relationships, the soft spots, the sore spots, the danger spots…they're all there. Actions have ramifications. A simple statement, but one with…well, large ramifications. This is a book about ramifications and about the difficulties of navigating the waters of responsibilities and relationships while attempting to remain mindful of the ramifications.

Time's Witness showed me what a good mystery is all about. Greed. Foibles. Loyalties. Duty. Choices… Ramifications. It is about imperfection. The basic framework of the mystery: someone is holding onto a secret and someone else is determined to reveal the secret, whatever the consequences.

Malone has already written the book I'd have loved to have written myself. Damn you, Malone! Then again, thank you. I've been doing my best ever since to write my own perfect mystery. With any luck, I'll never quite manage to pull it off. It's a far more energizing as a goal than the looking back on the task now completed. For my money, Michael Malone completed it. I have the luxury of looking back on his work and enjoying it over and over. Okay? Now it's your turn.

Tim Cockey is the award-winning author of five novels in the so-called "hearse series," including *The Hearse You Came In On*, *Murder in the Hearse Degree* and *Backstabber* (yes, it's a hearse book). He is also the author of the recently released *Speak of the Devil*, for which he has cloaked his identity under the guise of one Richard Hawke.

Twist Phelan on
Bootlegger's Daughter by Margaret Maron (1992)

As a new mystery writer — four years ago this winter I started my first book — I've been more influenced by what you might call "recent" classics, one in particular.

Margaret Maron's *Bootlegger's Daughter*, published in 1992, won the Edgar, Anthony, Agatha, and Macavity awards and was named one of the Independent Mystery Booksellers Association's 100 Favorite Mysteries of the Century. The first in a series featuring Deborah Knott, youngest child and only girl in a large family whose patriarch is a well-known bootlegger, the book opens when Deborah, now an attorney, decides to buck the good-ole-boy political machine and run for a local judgeship. Although busy drumming up votes and representing indigent clients, she agrees to look into a seventeen-year-old unsolved murder at the request of the victim's daughter, a friend since childhood. Deborah's efforts uncover long-buried secrets, putting her future, political and otherwise, at risk.

Set in a small rural town in North Carolina, where intricate and long-standing blood relationships are an important part of individual identity, *Bootlegger's Daughter* is as much a Southern novel of place and relationship as a murder mystery. In spare, straightforward prose that reflects the rhythms of the region, Maron looks at how big issues like race and class affect ordinary people, showing us that whatever goes on in the greater world, the little wrongs and moments of truth within a person's own universe can mean everything. I consider *Bootlegger's Daughter* a sort of family thriller. The pace may seem languid, but from page one we're caught up in the action, pulled into the lives of parents, siblings, cousins, aunts and uncles who are as endearing and annoying as our own.

This is what makes this book so memorable for me — the focus on conflict, internal and external, created in family situations. Maron gets it just right: family can be a haven in a scary world, but it's also a place where memory runs deep and feelings, high. Everyone knows everyone else, nothing is private — except those dark secrets that are never discussed, least of all by the people involved. The dreams, ambitions and shortcomings that make us most vulnerable are the very ones we try hardest to keep hidden from our relatives. Throw kin together in close quarters and true character emerges from the dense, complex web of dependencies and interdependencies. And unlike friends or business associates, family members aren't people you can give up and walk out on — you have to stick it out. Even if you do manage to leave, you never really separate: your family experience forever influences and informs you.

In writing my Pinnacle Peak mystery series, I am likewise drawn to an exploration of conflict and crime arising from family relationships. To me, domestic dynamics can be as complex as corporate shenanigans, as compelling a force as a high-rise fire or raging sea. Thanks to Margaret Maron, I felt able to set my stories not at the global level, but on a more intimate stage. *Bootlegger's Daughter* showed me that a tale of soul and malevolence can unfold just as powerfully around a dinner table as on the streets of Los Angeles or New York, and that a family setting can generate as much mystery and suspense as the most intricate spy mission.

Twist Phelan received her bachelor and law degrees from Stanford University. Success as a trial lawyer suing corporate scoundrels enabled her to retire in her early thirties. An avid athlete, Twist writes the Pinnacle Peak series, legal-themed mysteries each featuring a different sport. *Spurred Ambition* is her latest book.

Lea Wait on
She Walks These Hills by Sharyn McCrumb (1994)

Place and time as elements in fiction have always fascinated me.

In American mysteries, for example, often crimes which take place in Georgia could never have happened in northern Michigan, or in California. Crimes and family dynamics and even weapons take their clues from weather and seasons and social settings which differ dramatically across the country.

I write in two different genres. One of them plays with place, and one with time.

My novels for young people set in nineteenth century Maine are set in the small seacoast town of Wiscasset. In each book the main characters are faced with major decisions, at different points in history. But all the characters live in the same town, with the same river flowing to the east, the same northern hills lumbered or farmed. The sense of place that I hope infuses each book shows how climate and geography influence the actions and feelings of characters. (*Stopping to Home*, *Seaward Born* and *Wintering* are the first in this series, with *Finest Kind* to follow later in 2006.)

Time is important in my mystery series. Maggie Summer, the protagonist in the Shadows Antique Print Mystery series, is an antique print dealer and a community college professor. She finds clues to the solution of contemporary crimes in her eighteenth or nineteenth century prints. In *Shadows at the Fair,* she finds information in an old herbal which leads to an unusual pair of serial killers. In *Shadows on the Coast of Maine,* a home built in 1774 contains secrets and hides old crimes which set the stage for a murder in today's world. In *Shadows on the Ivy*, nineteenth century prints illuminate contradictions in American myths and lead Maggie to a killer who has created his own version of the "self-made man." In *Shadows in the Spring Show,* multi-cultural and multi-racial families connected to an antique show benefiting an adoption agency illustrate new interpretations of 19th century beliefs about anthropology.

Because place and time are so critical to my own writing, reading Sharyn McCrumb's *She Walks These Hills* was a revelation.

Not only does McCrumb knows her place — the hills of western North Carolina and eastern Kentucky — in depth, but she ignores the conventions about time that I assumed in my books. She doesn't write one novel about "now" and one novel about "then." In McCrumb's work, appearance and reality are the same.

The Appalachian hills are her protagonist. Because the hills have not changed, it is totally believable that Katie Wyler, who was captured by Indians in 1779 and followed the rivers through the wilderness back to her mountain home hundreds of miles away, should meet a lost and hungry twentieth century historian on a mountain pass, and that they both should encounter Harm Sorley, imprisoned in 1968 for murdering someone who poisoned the environment, and now trying to return to a family and home that no longer exist.

Elderly Nora Bonesteel, who "has the gift" and can see the past and the future as well as the present, knows better than to advertise her knowledge. But her existence reinforces what McCrumb illustrates: given a strong enough environment, the petty ways of men and women, their conflicts and their desires, their tragedies and their hopes, are all just a part of the stream of life.

I continue to reread and be impressed by Sharyn McCrumb's books, especially *She Walks These Hills*, and hope some day to approach the understanding of the American land, and its effect on the American people, that McCrumb depicts so brilliantly.

Lea Wait (www.leawait.com) writes the Shadows Antique

Print Mystery series: *Shadows at the Fair*, a finalist for a Best First Mystery Agatha; *Shadows on the Coast of Maine*; *Shadows on the Ivy*; and *Shadows After the Spring Show*. She also writes novels for ages eight to twelve set in nineteenth century Maine.

Larry D. Sweazy on
Breakheart Hill by Thomas Cook (1995)

From the first sentence to the last of Thomas H. Cook's novel, *Breakheart Hill*, I was confounded by what I was reading. Was it really a mystery novel? Could I categorize it in any of the subgenres? It certainly wasn't a police procedural or amateur sleuth novel, nor was it a cozy or a hardboiled novel. But it did have all of the elements of a mystery.

Detection lies at the heart of the novel with the unrelenting search for the truth always at the forefront. The suspense is tight and ever present with the plot and character revelations unfolding slowly, urging the reader to keep asking: what really happened to Kelli Troy on Breakheart Hill? There is a red herring, or multiple red herrings, depending on how one wants to look it at. And there is a quantifiable, horrific crime — along with a trial and conviction of the main suspect.

When I began to seriously analyze the plot of *Breakheart Hill*, I found it simple, familiar and expertly devised. It is a small town view of the early 1960s in the South, painfully experiencing desegregation mixed with adolescent love, unrequited love, reflected back on by a middle-aged doctor. The structure of the plot, shuffling from present to the past, and back again, in the easy, pained voice of the doctor, Ben Wade, is built with such ease that it was tempting to read this novel in one sitting. But a quick read would not allow the reader to savor the nuances of time, and form the larger view that Cook has constructed.

Ben Wade was in love with Kelli Troy, a beautiful high school girl who moved with her mother to Choctaw from Baltimore. The love is not returned by Kelli in the way Ben hoped it would be. Kelli is more taken with Todd Jeffries, Romeo to her Juliet in the school play. Kelli is aghast at the prejudice she sees and experiences in Choctaw, and is verbally assaulted days before her tragic accident by Lyle Gates, who ultimately goes to prison for Kelli's demise. After years of searching, of knowing there was more to Kelli's fate than anyone ever knew, Ben Wade finally discovers the truth, and his own culpability in the crime. Justice is served in the end, not on a legal level, but on a moral level, as it is so many times in real life and in any good mystery.

So, I concluded, days after setting the book aside, that *Breakheart Hill* really is a mystery novel. One that celebrates all of the elements of the genre, while reaching beyond the confines of publishing standards with heart and good writing, making it nothing more than an excellent story that stays with the reader long after it has been put on the shelf.

As a writer, *Breakheart Hill* opened up a new path for me. The novel demanded that I look beyond the categories and focus solely on the interior and exterior lives of all of the characters. It demanded that I tell the truth, and demanded, finally, that to be a good writer, I must get to the heart of the matter without concern for anything else other than telling a good story.

Larry D. Sweazy's short story, "The Promotion," won the Western Writers of America 2005 Spur award for best short fiction, and also appeared in *The Adventure of the Missing Detective And 25 of the Year's Finest Crime and Mystery Stories!* He lives in Indiana, and is a fulltime freelance indexer.

Pari Noskin Taichert on
What's the Worst That Could Happen? by Donald E.
Westlake (1996)

The way I remember it, the sky was as dark as my mood. Another rejection letter sat on my desk, crumpled and crippling. My computer hummed, but the noise droned without distinction. Inspiration flowed through someone else's fingertips.

In desperation, I went to the library and wandered amid the bookcases feeling sorry for myself. Mumbling, I composed never-to-be-sent responses to agents and editors who scorned the brilliance of my manuscripts. Surrounded by books, I pouted. Why did other people get published, anyway?

After awhile, I arrived at the Ws in the fiction section — and saw it. There, at eye level, sat a novel taunting and tempting with its innocent title, *What's the Worst that Could Happen?*

Donald Westlake's use of six common words to hint at grand misadventure brought laughter and despair like one-two punches to my literary ego and compositional laziness. He lured me in before I had even opened his book. Though the intentionality of the title impressed me, I was in no mood to be won over.

Unconvinced, I picked up the book between two fingers — as if it might burn — and skimmed. A quick paragraph about gaudy boutiques with shiny thises and thats and then this line, "It was like being in a duty-free shop for magpies."

How could I not fall in love with Westlake's voice then and there? His ability to capture moments and translate them into something fresh on the page unleashed a seminal realization. Even the most ordinary plot can sparkle anew when an author takes the time to craft what I now call "zingers." These deceptively brief observations or lines of dialog are the stuff of great reads, the spicy snaps of perfectly wrought scenes.

Reading *What's the Worst that Could Happen?* is like watching a seasoned storyteller, the kind that sets up a scene without anyone realizing it and concludes with a punch line — or moral — that is unanticipated but natural, seamless.

That Westlake is able to achieve this in humorous fiction attests to his astounding craft. Writing humor is a tricky business. What one person thinks is funny may not tickle another. One of the main dangers is overdoing it, trying too hard to come up with the wry observation or turn of phrase. When that happens, it's too obvious and the story becomes a parody of itself, a dud.

When I read Donald Westlake's *What's the Worst that Could Happen?* for the first time, I found myself grinning. Those grins turned into full-face smiles that, in turn, became chuckles. I enjoyed the ride with increasing satisfaction and knew it was because of something unidentifiable, like a spice that complements everything in a dish so perfectly you can't pick it out.

I studied *What's the Worst that Could Happen?* and began to discover the tell-tale signs of the author's technique. Westlake's zingers hit softly at first, but accumulated. Every page of the book had them quietly waiting to gratify readers, to add to the pleasure of the experience.

Since that day in the library, I've met many Westlake fans. They adore the Dortmunder series for the inevitable disasters its namesake creates, faces, and overcomes. The plotting is convoluted, wonderful and, somehow, believable. But for me, it's the little things that count.

Westlake and *What's the Worst that Could Happen?* inspired me to try harder as a writer, to eschew smugness. I'm convinced I never would have been published without this push to bring something special — through zingers — to every page of my work.

What's the Worst that Could Happen? was the best thing that could happen to me.

Pari Noskin Taichert hails from Albuquerque, lived in wetter climes, and had the smarts to return home. She is the author of two Agatha Award-nominated novels: *The Clovis Incident* (Best First, 2004) and *The Belen Hitch* (Best Novel, 2005). Unlike her protagonist, Sasha Solomon, Pari is married, has children and leads a normal life.

Michael Koryta on
Gone, Baby, Gone by Dennis Lehane (1998)

Walk through the door of my office, and you'll find yourself facing four bookshelves, several hundred books scattered among them. Your eyes will probably focus first on a set of Dennis Lehane hardcovers placed on an eye-level shelf by design, not by accident. I want to see those books each time I go to my desk to write for two reasons: I want to remember what got me started in this business, and, more importantly, I want to remember where the bar is set.

Gone, Baby, Gone represents those things. All of Lehane's work does, really, but to me, that one is special. It was the first Lehane novel I read, and it had a more profound impact on me than any other book. I can remember finding it — bottom shelf of a small collection of mystery paperbacks in Howard's Bookstore in my hometown. I was sixteen years old, looking for something to read for a weekend trip. A review quote caught my eye — "The hippest heir to Chandler and Hammett," it said. I skimmed the synopsis — skimmed it so disinterestedly that when I started the book I was surprised to find Patrick's partner was a woman — and took it to the cash register. I don't remember a whole lot of excitement over the purchase, or even a particularly high amount of interest in the book. I needed something to read, and that one had found its way into my hand, that was all. I'm eternally grateful it did.

Gone, Baby, Gone captivated me from its haunting opening sentence: "Each day in this country, twenty-three hundred children are reported missing." Halfway through the book, I began to really appreciate what I was experiencing as a reader — I was in the hands of a master. A *new* master. Is there any more exciting find than that? Lehane's writing captured place and character as well as anything I'd ever read, moved a powerful plot while subtly addressing the world we live in, told a gripping detective story that was at the same time about so much more than that detective story. I finished the book in two days and set it aside. I think it sat for about 24 hours before I picked it up and read it all over again. I was utterly blown away by what I'd seen: a writer who could produce a suspense novel full of all the thrills and action of the genre's best, yet leave behind a haunting question of morality and social conscience.

In the next few weeks of that spring, I read every book Dennis had written — at that time it was four; *Prayers for Rain* came out that summer while *Mystic River*, which would turn the genre on its ear, was still in the works. I read them all, and then I read them all again. And again. I'd always wanted to write, and I'd always enjoyed mysteries and crime fiction, but it had been a passing interest, an "I might give that a shot someday" outlook until I found *Gone, Baby, Gone*. By the time I finished the Patrick Kenzie/Angela Genarro series, the passing interest had become a compulsion. There was no other course for me now — I was going to write, and I was going to write in this genre.

Six years after discovering Lehane, my first book was published, and one of my first signings was at Howard's Bookstore. I sat maybe four feet from where I'd found *Gone, Baby, Gone,* and at one point in the night I looked over and gave that bottom shelf a slight salute. In a similar gesture, *Gone, Baby, Gone* and its companion books will remain on that eye-level shelf in my office, hopefully joined by new Lehane volumes soon enough, to remind me why I'm writing, and to remind me of the standard I'm chasing.

Michael Koryta's first novel, *Tonight I Said Goodbye*, was published when he was just 21. This first book featuring PI Lincoln Perry won two awards, was nominated for the Edgar for best first novel, and has been translated into several languages. He is a native of Bloomington, Indiana.

Index

Bold page references indicate a contributing author.